GOLF PRACTICE

GOLF PRACTICE

HOW TO PRACTICE GOLF AND TAKE YOUR RANGE GAME TO THE COURSE

by Iain Highfield and Team Game Like Training -
Matthew Cooke, Arick Zeigel & Zach Parker

Copyright © 2019 by Iain Highfield

All rights reserved. No part of this book may be reproduced or transmitted in any form or by any means, electronic or mechanical, including photocopying, recording, or any information storage and retrieval system, without permission in writing from the author.

ISBN: 978-0-9992667-3-1 - Paperback
eISBN: 978-0-9992667-4-8 - ePub
eISBN: 978-0-9992667-5-5 - mobi

Printed in the United States of America   1 2 0 4 1 9

∞This paper meets the requirements of ANSI/NISO Z39.48-1992 (Permanence of Paper)

*Thanks to Dr Tim Lee, Dr Anders Ericsson and Len Hill PHD for their
inspiration and guidance on the science of learning and human performance.*

Many thanks to Andrew Boulton for his edits and making the words on our original transcript sing.

Many thanks to Romell Greene for his graphic design and making our original images dance.

CONTENTS

1 – Welcome to the GLT Tribe 1

2 – Training to Learn 7

3 – Training to Learn: Practical Application 15

4 – Training to Perform 47

5 – Training to Perform: Practical Application 57

6 – Motivation Trumps All, While Confidence Can Be A Killer 83

7 – Making PAR 87

1 – Golf Practice
Welcome to the GLT Tribe

Simply by holding this book in your hands, you have joined an adventure that began in 2010 at Cookridge Hall golf club in Leeds, England. Based on their formal education and observations of how golf was being coached, Iain Highfield and Matthew Cooke embarked on a mission to help educate and inspire the golfing world to do two pretty important things. Think Differently and Train Differently.

As you read this book, a ridiculous number of fellow golfers all over the world are engaging in **sum zero training** (which is basically training that doesn't actually help anyone learn to play better golf). And those same golfers are also probably pondering the oldest (and, weirdly, most easily answerable) question in golf:

> 'Why, why, why, why, why (etc.)
> can't I take my range game to the golf course?'

The answer to this question (admittedly one that the **Game Like Training** team has spent a decade trying to solve) is a framework that helps coaches and players think and practice in a way that will lead to the **retention and transfer** of golfing skill.

We've accumulated thousands of hours coaching golf at all levels, studying sports psychology, the learning sciences and – most importantly – spending time with some of the greatest minds in, not only professional golf, but also many other fields of human performance. And what that has given us (apart from significantly less hair than we used to) is a distillation of this vast bank of knowledge that makes it practical (and digestible) for you to become a better golfer where, and when, it matters most.

'Rather than reasoning by analogy you boil things down to the most fundamental truths you can imagine, and you reason up from there. This will help you figure out if something really makes sense.' Elon Musk

Following in the footsteps of old Musky, our decade of investigating, learning and investigating some more has led us to our fundamental golfing truth:

'learning happens via **cognitive stress**'

So, again with a little inspiration from the Musketeer, we 'reasoned up' from this truth. In other words, we asked what actually creates that fundamental state of cognitive stress. The answer…

spacing, variability and **challenge**

The Spacing Effect

To forget is to remember.

Now, even though this may seem like the kind of empty, pseudo-zen nonsense you'll see written over pictures of sunsets – it's a central pillar of human learning.

By incorporating the spacing effect to your training, you are effectively increasing the time you take between each rep.

This creates cognitive stress as your brain – or more specifically, your working memory – is challenged to recall previous successful reps (more so than if there is little or no time between shots). So, rather than simply machine-gunning balls down the range, you are actively teaching your brain to induce a deeper degree of learning,

A very basic example of this could be instead of hitting the same shot 20 times in a row as fast as you can, limiting yourself to hitting 1 ball a minute for 20 minutes – which, admittedly, may sound like a nightmare to range-ragers.

The Variability Effect

Some significant neurobiological research from Stanford University has provided a bit of bad news for the way most people practice golf – namely, the evidence that suggests our brains need variety if we are going to learn.

In other, more golfy, terms, learning through repetition is, in most scenarios, ineffective.

Instead, constantly changing the nature and application of tasks is vital for successfully learning and mastering any new movement – such as a golf swing – as this conscious variance is far better when it comes to engaging memory recall and creating cognitive stress.

So, rather than hitting 20 balls with the same club to the same target, the variability effect demands that you mix things up – changing your club and target regularly and repeatedly.

The Optimal Challenge Point

Increasing the spacing and variability in your practice will in turn increase the challenge point it presents. So, the more space and variability your training contains the higher the challenge point – and the more purposeful and rewarding that practice session has become.

Setting outcome goals is another way to elevate your own challenge point – with more complex and testing self-targeting representing a higher challenge point.

If we combine some of the scenarios from our spacing and variability effects, and embellish it with outcome goals we have already created the conditions of cognitive stress.

So, for example…

If we hit 20 balls in 20 minutes

AND we change our club and our target every two balls

AND we award ourselves with a point every time the ball is struck from the center of the club face

AND if we set ourselves a target to achieve 14 points within those 20 balls

THEN we are in the state of cognitive stress and therefore, a state of learning

Make Sense?

The next stage in the Elon Musk method is to recognize whether the fundamental truth we are exploring makes sense.

For us, it absolutely did, largely because it creates what is known in the learning sciences as **contextual interference**. This interference (manifesting through factors like the time between each shot, changing of club or differing lies) is responsible for the memory improvement that aids learning.

And if you want to retain and transfer golfing skill (something that most golfers fail to do hence the *'I can't take my range game to the course'* complaint) then you need context to build the mental representations that help you adapt to the most demanding golfing environments.

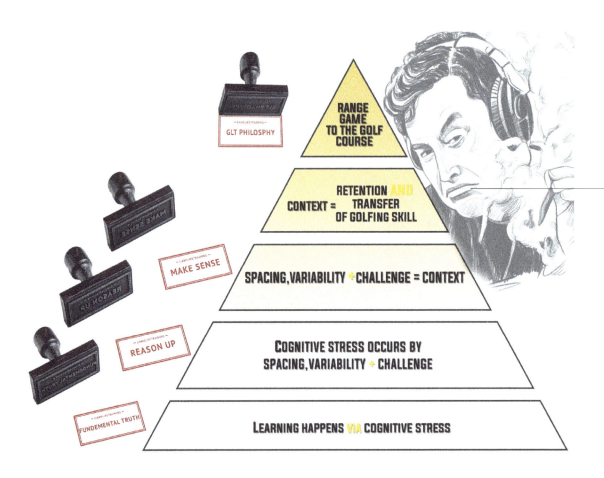

4 | Game Like Training

Who Are We Talking to

If you are a club golfer who wants to lower your handicap, a junior golfer that wants to gain representative honors, a mini tour player that wants to step up a league or even if you are already at the elite level but are striving for more… this book will help you.

Our aim is pretty simple. In fact, we only really want to show you two things…

What
type of interaction has to happen between the brain, body and the environment for golfers to acquire new skills.

And (probably more importantly)

How
you can practice at home, on the range or the course in a way that will bring you closer to achieving your golfing goals.

And, in return, we only need you to do one thing: **practice.**

What We Talk About When We Talk About Practice

At Game Like Training we see deliberate practice as part of a continuum that is designed to fuel **game-like** repetitions. (Spoiler alert, that's why we called our company **Game Like Training**.)

But no, at Game Like Training we are not simply playing games. We are using frameworks such as 'teaching games for understanding' and 'challenge point' to design specific tasks for golfers that create an optimal learning environment – built around their physical, mental, technical and performance needs.

The conclusion of this process is when maximum contextual interference has been introduced, the player is building mental representations that recreate and simulate the game of golf.

In other words, the GLT process may begin on the golf range but it certainly does not end there. (And that, as they say, is kinda the point.)

So, with deliberate, game-like practice in our hearts and on our business cards, you won't be surprised to hear that the aim for this book is to a.) help you practice more effectively but also b.) help you walk away from the habits and dogma that holds players back from improving their game.

We won't lie, this book could be classed by some as 'sciencey' – and it is, but only in the sense that we have taken all the most relevant contemporary research and theories and applied them to every kind of golfer, playing at every level, under every type of professional or personal restrictions.

In other words, whether you're able to practice 2 hours a week or 40 hours a week we have structured this book in a way that can be adapted to your lifestyle and ability level.
There is value in these pages, and the path to a better game, for anyone who is willing to practice and (more importantly) willing to step outside their comfort zone and practice golf the GLT way.

So, every time we tell you about a training strategy that can induce deeper learning, we will also give you specific, practical training tasks with different levels depending on your own ability and experience.

Now's the time to say goodbye to the comfort zone and see how the GLT team can help you train differently and think about your game in a way you never have before.

GLT x

2 – Golf Practice
Training to Learn

When a golfer turns up to practice they should ask themselves one vital question:

'Am I training to learn or am I training to perform?'

For the purpose of this book we will class **training to learn** as stimulating the connections in the brain that help you learn to move the club in a desired motion. Scientists may call this synaptogenesis.

Training to perform, in these pages at least, is about finding ways to adapt to the environmental demands and psychological stresses of the golf course and competition. Performance experts would suggest players who can do this can access a state of 'flow'.

So, as we try to enhance your ability to learn golfing movements and flow in competition, let's start by trampling over one of golf's many unhelpful training myths.

Myth...
Repetition leads to better swings and better scores

If this news has unsettled you (we know plenty of golfers and coaches who would sooner burn their bag than listen to this sort of heresy) let's think about it in another way.

Imagine being in school and the teacher asking you the following sequence of questions, **5+5=? and 5+5=? and 5+5=? and 5+5=? and 5+5=? and 5+5=?** Even as a child you would suspect this type of math test is not making you a great deal brighter.

We've already touched on the limitations of mere repetition – namely the absence of spacing, variability, challenge and, of course, cognitive stress.

Simply put, it's too easy, yet this is precisely what many golfers are habitually, even ritually, doing as 'practice'.

Blocked practice

Blocked practice is basically when you repeat the same task over and over in the same manner, under the same stresses and conditions.

It can actually be a really useful tool for beginners, as they learn the unfamiliar movements and interactions of posture, grip and even just getting a golf ball into the air.

But as soon as you are hoping to learn and develop anything approaching an advanced skill, blocked practice is actually a barrier to that learning.

The GLT definition of a truly learned golf skill is one that is retained over time and transferred into multiple environments.

Skills acquired through blocked practice are not typically retained for any significant period of time and rarely transfer easily.

So, for a player to 'learn' golfing skill in line with the GLT definition, those skills need to be developed through practice structured in what's called an **interleaved** manner.

Interleaved Practice

While blocked practice involves only one task being completed thoroughly before moving to another, interleaving is a process where students mix, or interleave, multiple practice tasks in order to improve their learning.

It's designed to challenge golfers to access and complete **motor processes**, the commands by which humans use their brain to activate and coordinate the muscles and limbs involved in the performance of a **motor** skill, such as a golf swing.

So, by stopping you from simply repeating the same task for a short-term performance gain, interleaved practice creates a cognitive and physical relationship with what you are practicing.

To better illustrate its effect, think back again to school and cramming for an exam. How many of those last-minute facts about Thomas Jefferson or cumulus clouds can you recall now?

Unless you're currently a historian or meteorologist, we'd imagine not a lot, probably because the way you attempted to develop that retention was too blocked, and therefore not robust enough to last.

By forcing golfers to self-diagnose and complete motor processes, interleaved practice makes us our own best coach, as solutions to the total problem of hitting a golf shot are self-discovered.

Through interleaved practice, players not only retain what they learn much longer, they increase the chance of those learnings transferring onto the golf course.

Motor Learning

At the heart of virtually every golf skill is the **motor system**.

This is a component of the central nervous system that drives the actions of muscles on bones and joints, resulting in movement – which is incredibly smart.

It's got a lot to do with swing technique, something players spend countless hours trying to master – which is less smart.

As you can now imagine, golf skills involve much more than that. We use sensory information to decide what to do before a shot is made, conscious human assessments like reading the break of a putt. We also use sensory information during the swing to control movement, such as the length and tempo of a putting stroke, to determine the correct speed.

We rely on our cognitive system to make good decisions, carefully aiming away from those dreaded out-of-bounds posts and water hazards.

So, when we perform and learn golf skills, we are using much more than the 'motor' component. So much so that, in the context of golf 'motor learning' is actually better described as 'perceptual-sensory-motor-cognitive learning' (which admittedly isn't quite as punchy so we'll stick here to calling it motor learning).

What motor learning absolutely is not is a process of ingraining something in 'muscle memory'. This is mostly because muscle memory does not actually exist. (Yep, despite what athletics commentators at the Olympics love to shout through your TV, muscles do not have memories.)

So if the goal of practice is not to create muscle memory, it must be to create the motor learning a golfer needs to execute a single shot through a series of interconnected elements. In other words, effective practice means *practicing the entire process*.

And, if we are practicing the entire process, we come back again to interleaved practice, which encourages us to not simply work on the shot, but the *process* of hitting the shot.

Feedback

In the last decade there have been some extraordinary advances in what we understand about the way people learn. This information and evidence is freely available, and could be picked up by any golfer or coach in the world and used to enhance their performance.

The key to the ever-elusive transfer between range practice and course performance is there for everyone to access, providing us all with probably the single most important strategy for taking your game to the next level.

At the heart of this are the state of cognitive stress and the three components needed to replicate it – spacing, variability, challenge. And, unsurprisingly, it is interleaved practice that does the best job of allowing these factors to present themselves while we train.

Interleaved practice can also be key in creating effective use of training aids and providing a golfer with the right amounts and types of developmental **feedback**.

Golf has always had a rather affectionate relationship with feedback. Golfers love advice, be it from a trained professional, a friend, or from a stranger in the next bay at the driving range. Sometimes it helps, sometimes it does not and sometimes it makes things worse.

But, what defines the quality and value of feedback is in the difference between the various sources of information.

We call it **augmented feedback** when the information comes from an outside source, like an instructor, video, launch monitor, or even a training aid. And we call it **inherent feedback** when it arises from within, such as seeing, feeling or hearing information.

Here's an example of why this difference is significant. If we were to try and remember when we first heard someone say our down swing was 'over the top' and had resulted in a slice across the ball, we'd probably recall that we had no idea what the term meant, what this looked like, or why it would result in a slice across the ball.

In this case, augmented feedback would be critical to learning about the 'over the top' swing – and how to reduce this movement or replace it with a desired one.

For example, verbal feedback helps us understand this new term and to visualize the solution. Video feedback could also help us understand what our arms and body were doing during the down swing. A golf training aid might be used to prevent us from making an over the top swing next time.

Without question, these sources of augmented feedback will help you make corrections on the range. But, as we all know, the errors we correct on the range sometimes return to haunt us on the course. And remember, none of those sources of augmented feedback are available to the golfer on the course. So, how can you optimize the use of augmented feedback in practice in order to improve your play on the course? Basically, we limit it.

Information from an external source such as a teaching professional, a launch monitor, a video, or even a training aid can serve to highlight information to the golfer that would otherwise go undetected. The information can also go a long way to helping the golfer to make corrections.

But there is a down side to augmented feedback, too. Motor learning research has found that augmented feedback can have a negative effect on the golfer when it becomes a 'crutch' for error detection and correction. A crutch that may do a grand job of propping you up on the golf range, but gets whipped away and leaves you tumbling into a bunker as soon as you step onto the course.

Research into the 'crutch' effect has found that when participants are presented with augmented feedback after every practice attempt, their performance on a retention test is worse than when compared participants who received the same feedback every 10 balls.

The explanation for these findings is simple. Receiving augmented feedback too often, too soon or in such a way that it *guides* the golfer towards understanding the nature of the error and how to correct it, becomes a liability when the learner must later perform in the absence of that augmented feedback. This guidance role of augmented feedback prevents the golfer from learning to use inherent sources to obtain the same information.

Reducing the **guidance** effect of augmented feedback, by reducing its frequency, enhances performance as it encourages the learner to rely more upon their inherent sources of feedback – sources of feedback that will be available later in retention and transfer tests and for the competitive golfers amongst us, the only source of feedback you can legally use on the golf course during competition.

Blocked practice can encourage golfers to rely too heavily on training aids and guidance devices, which in turn end up providing too much augmented feedback.
Interleaving practice, however, provides the opportunity to make augmented feedback optimal, reducing the frequency of the training aid's intervention.

One other fact that you may not immediately enjoy, but will absolutely come to embrace, is that interleaving practice will lead to an increase in errors compared to blocked practice.

This is because the training devices are removed as you switch between tasks or drills – meaning the guidance effect is being reduced which, in turn, causes more errors.

Don't Worry

These errors actually help you to learn more effectively, withholding the 'crutch' of augmented feedback and encouraging you to search for your own solutions or inherent feedback.

Just like a good coach knows when to be quiet and allow a golfer to actively discover solutions, a good practice session knows when to remove a training aid and attempt to learn through inherent feedback.

So, while error terror is a real and debilitating phenomenon, we need you to remember this…

1. Making a mistake in practice does not teach you how to make mistakes

2. Making errors in practice actually makes it more likely you will avoid those errors on the course

3. Errors are a golden opportunity to learn, embrace every one

Time to practice

Now, with great excitement – the kind of excitement usually reserved for when Tiger's in the final group of a Sunday – Team GLT have got some interleaved practice circuits that will help you experiment with spacing, variability, challenge and the opportunity to experience inherent feedback. Please, do a quick Tiger fist pump and turn the page.

Golf Practice | 13

3 – Golf Practice
Training to Learn: Practical Application

Imagine this, you go to the doctor with an ailment (we won't ask what). He uses some remarkable technology to diagnose your complaint and then announces what's wrong. Following this process there is an awkward silence before he asks you to leave his office. No advice on how to get better, no prescription, just the deeply unsettling knowledge of how you are unwell.

This analogy is present in golf teaching every day. Golfers across the globe visit a teacher and, using the latest technology, are given a diagnosis of what is wrong with their swing – but no prescription on how they can cure it.

There may be some information provided that's roughly the equivalent of our doctor saying *'you have a cold, so you probably need to sneeze and cough less'*. But prescriptions that lead to lasting change are few and far between in the golf world.

OK, we are being unfair, this is a vast generalization.

Golf coaches from all generations have incredible knowledge on many aspects of the sport, particularly on the mechanics of the golf swing. The understanding of what has to happen as the club travels around the body is so comprehensive that it frankly leaves us stunned.

But there is undeniably an absence in even the most advanced technical training – the small matter of 'how'. Or, more specifically, how do players practice in a way that helps them make lasting change to their motion?

The following practice tasks will help you – whether player, coach or both – apply the strategy of interleaving into the way you practice, helping you use the range in a way that dramatically increases the chance of retaining golfing skills.

And don't worry if you can't squeeze in a visit to the range, we've even created a few practice circuits that can be done in the comfort of your own home. In other words, there are no excuses.

Amongst this wide range of challenges, your job is to find the ones that most effectively create the optimal levels of spacing, variability and challenge for you.

For a beginner, the spacing, variability and challenge you build into your practice can start at a fairly low level, whereas professionals should be looking to keep these factors as high as possible for the following tasks.

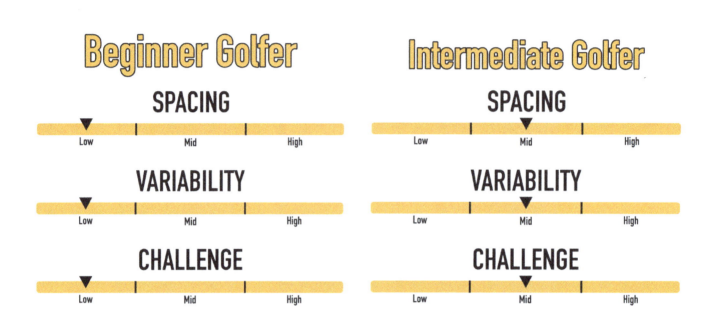

16 | Game Like Training

Fundamentals Practice

Here at GTL our motto is, if in doubt, give a definition – so here's what we mean when we talk about a fundamental:

Forming a necessary base or core of central importance

And while we absolutely agree that the stance, grip and posture fall into this category, it remains a highly individualized relationship.

The grip, for example, must match the player's release pattern, their posture must match their physical capability, their body and the stance must align with the environment in which the shot will be hit in, and so on.

Our time with some of the world's best coaches has helped us recognize the fundamentals of any player's swing is likely to be less prescribed qualities such as their balance, tempo, tension and center-face contact.

So, when we talk about developing the fundamentals, we're talking about developing a set of skills and behaviors that go way beyond how you stand and where your thumb sits.

A little note before you start…

The spacing, variability and challenge for all the following circuits have been set by our team at the optimal level to help induce deeper learning – or, more importantly, to make your positive swing changes stick.

And remember, the drills you're about to see may not all be the right ones for you. One of the GLT coaches has selected them based on their professional experiences and beliefs, not based on knowing you as an individual or golfer. Please feel free to replace these drills with something equivalent from your coach or PGA professional.

Practice Circuit 1 – Balance Circuit

The goal – This circuit is designed to help you, develop an understanding of what a more balanced set-up and golf swing feels like.

What to Do

Drill 1 – Eyes Closed
Make 2-4 practice swings and then hit 1 shot with your eyes closed (preferably with golf shoes off).

Drill 2 – Toe Up
Make 1 practice swing and hit 1 ball with the toes of your trail foot lifted off the ground as high as you can. This would be the right foot for a right-handed golfer, or the left foot for a left-handed golfer. You should feel like you're curling your toes up towards the sky.

Drill 3 – Jump Drill

Address the golf ball in full golf posture. Jump in the air (as high as you want) and as you land notice how you naturally settle into a more balanced and athletic stance. Once you have created this solid base or platform, hit the shot.

To view these drills in action and get some additional ideas on how to add spacing, variability, and challenge to your "training to learn" practice, visit – https://youtu.be/uQQfsbZbJZA

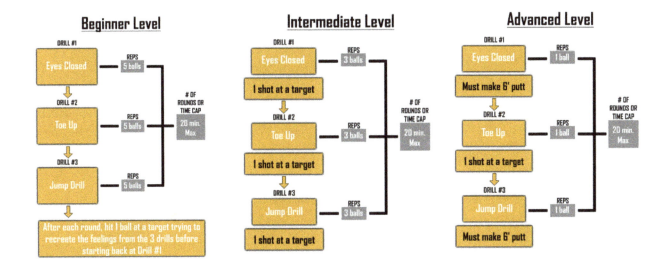

Golf Practice | 19

Practice Circuit 2 – Tempo Circuit

The goal – This circuit helps you develop an understanding of your best tempo – which has a direct impact on swing mechanics.

What To Do

Drill 1 – Speed Progression
This drill is a 5-ball set:

Hit ball 1 at 20% of your normal swing speed

Hit ball 2 at 40% of your normal swing speed

Hit ball 3 at 60% of your normal swing speed

Hit ball 4 at 80% of your normal swing speed

Hit ball 5 at 100% of your normal swing speed

Drill 2 – Counting
Make practice swings counting upwards from 1 as you set to the ball. Once you feel you have a connection between the numbers and the swing hit a shot.

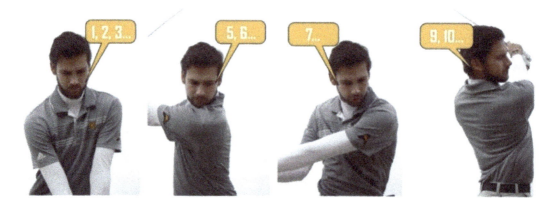

Drill 3 – Transition Awareness

Hit 1 ball taking the club away as fast as you can and then hit 1 ball taking the club away as slow as you can. Hit 1 more ball picking a takeaway speed that you feel leads to the best tempo.

To view these drills in action and get some additional ideas on how to add spacing, variability, and challenge to your "training to learn" practice, visit - https://youtu.be/EqbI_KO3d-s

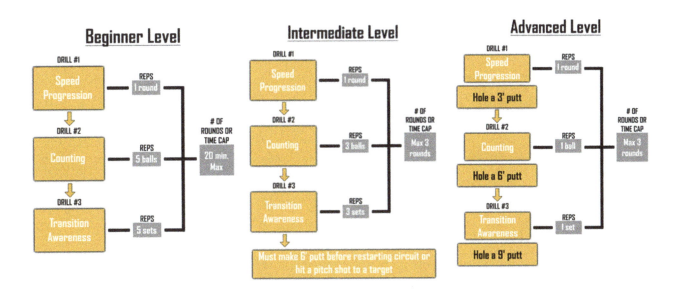

Practice Circuit 3 – Tension Circuit

The goal – This circuit helps develop tension awareness – and understand more about how the tension in your hands, shoulder and jaw can impact your swing mechanics.

What To Do

Drill 1 – Tension Awareness

Take your normal grip on the golf club. Breathe in, and then exhale, and when you feel relaxed squeeze the grip as tightly as you can.

Maintain this tense grip pressure for a few seconds and then slowly release the tension.

Repeat this process 3 times and then grip the club with a tension level that feels comfortable.

While maintaining the grip pressure, make a practice swing.

Then, when you're ready, hit a ball – all the while keeping your chosen grip pressure the same.

Drill 2 – High Soft Lob Shot

Take your most lofted club and make a full swing – but as softly and slowly as possible.

The goal is to hit a full shot, but for the ball to go as short a distance as possible – forcing you to be mindful of the mass of the club as well as any unwanted tension within your body.
(Imagine if you were to swing a rope, how soft and relaxed that would feel and look.)

Drill 3 – Right Arm Only

Take your six iron and hit a shot with your right arm only.

The purpose of this is again to gain awareness of the mass of the club and how it wants to move around your body naturally.

You should be able to feel signs of unwanted tension, if you're struggling to make solid contact.

To view these drills in action and get some additional ideas on how to add spacing, variability, and challenge to your "training to learn" practice, visit – https://youtu.be/yEfT3lRXS0w

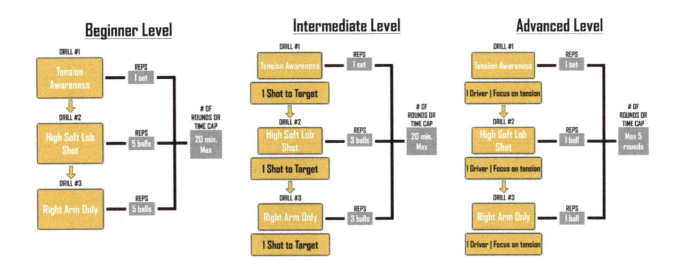

Golf Practice | 23

Practice Circuit 4 – Contact Tester

The Goal

This circuit helps you understand and adapt your club delivery (and retain this ability) when faced with varying lies you are likely to experience out on the course.

What To Do

Beginner

Place 5 balls on differing tee heights.

Hit all 5 balls giving yourself 1 point every time you strike the ball cleanly.

Repeat 4 times (total of 20 balls) and record your best score.

Intermediate

Place 3 balls on differing tee heights.

Hit all 3 balls with the goal of hitting them in the center of the face.

Then hit 2 balls from the ground giving yourself a point if you hit the ball in the center of the face.

Repeat 5 times (total of 25 balls) and record your best score.

Advanced

Place 3 balls on differing tee heights.

Hit all 3 balls with the goal of hitting them in the center of the face.

Then hit 2 balls from the ground giving yourself a point if you hit BOTH balls in the center of the face.

Repeat 4 times (total of 20 balls) and if you do not achieve at least 3 points, you must repeat the challenge.

To view these drills in action and get some additional ideas on how to add spacing, variability, and challenge to your "training to learn" practice, visit – https://youtu.be/uvcOkjHyet8

Swing Practice

Coaching the complete spectrum of players has also helped us develop an understanding of not only the most common barriers and faults, but *how* players can train to create sustainable swing changes to address these issues.

The word 'fix' is a dirty word when it comes to golf practice. To fix something implies that we're somehow fastening or securing it to an immoveable point.

This is, of course, absolutely fine if we are talking engines and cars. But it's a principle that does not translate into human beings swinging golf clubs.

A coach who claims they can fix your swing is the golf equivalent of those fitness campaigns that try to persuade us that some oiled and chiseled beauty 'lost 300lbs in 30 days without dieting or exercising'.

At GLT we don't ever attempt to fix a golf swing. Our intervention comes through deliberate engagement in the sort of practice circuits you're about to experience. The aim being, not to fix, mend or correct but to induce sustainable motor learning via the creation of cognitive stress.

Understandably, this takes a great deal of time and effort. In fact, if you've ever heard the saying **'when we fire, we wire'** you can imagine just how many times our old swing pattern has been fired – and therefore wired into our cognitive behaviors.

There is no quick fix to not only undo that old motor program, but also engineer a new one. That's why you need to be prepared to put time and effort, not into perusing some snake-oil, swing-fix miracle, but into creating new synapses in your brain.

Which, handily, is what we're about to show you how to achieve.

Practice Circuit 5 – Eliminate The Dreaded Slice

The Goal

This circuit will focus on your clubface control both in the transition and throughout impact – helping you learn how to make swing compensations to keep your club face square and avoid a pull slice.

What To Do

Drill 1 – Transition Drill
Go to the top of your backswing, pause and try to feel your lead wrist bow – the action which will close the clubface

Rotate your body through, trying to hit a push draw.

The key is to feel your wrist bowing while starting the downswing, without any pulling on the grip – instead, you should only feel a smooth bowing and the lower body rotation that initiates the downswing.

Drill 2 – Fleetwood Finish
Understanding how to rotate your upper body and stabilize the club face through impact is the goal of this drill.

To do this, we want to create an abbreviated finish for each rep, where your upper body has created the speed and your arms can stop without any recoil.

When done correctly your arms and body should be synchronized, resulting in a smooth, balanced finish position.

Drill 3 – Alignment Rod Start Line Drill

Place an alignment rod nine feet in front of your ball, directly on your intended target line.

(Using the rod as an external focus allows your body to unlock the information needed for the club delivery at impact.)

The aim now is for each struck ball to start to the right of the alignment rod and draw.

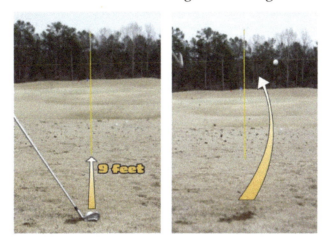

To view these drills in action and get some additional ideas on how to add spacing, variability, and challenge to your "training to learn" practice, visit – https://youtu.be/ppyVOpXtv7g

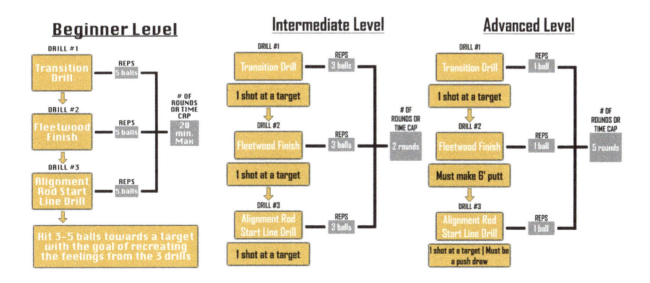

Golf Practice | 29

Practice Circuit 6 – Stop The Pull Hook

The Goal

To help you develop a better understanding of the body's role in how to eliminate the pull hook – as well as generate processes that can be taken into play on the golf course.

What To Do

Drill 1 – Lead Arm Priming Drill
No golf club is needed for this drill.

Take your stance and rotate your arms so that the palms of your hands are facing away from you.

Rotate your lead arm, keeping your shoulder back.

Your trail arm will follow and stop where the ball would be.

Repeat this motion slowly and deliberately 5 times and then hit 1 golf ball.

Drill 2 – Right Arm Structure Drill
Pick a club and set up to a golf ball.

Start your back swing and stop just as the club reaches parallel to the ground (image 2) and make sure the head of the club is inside the hands.

Then rotate towards the golf ball, keeping your right arm in the same place all the way through impact.

Hit one ball at a low speed, really focusing on maintaining the right arm position as you rotate through the ball.

Drill 3 – Gate Challenge

Place 2 alignment rods 2ft apart and 8ft in front of you, creating a gateway.

Holding on to the feelings from drill 1 and drill 2, attempt to hit the ball through the gate.

(If you are a beginner golfer, you can choose to hit the ball to the right of the gate. Intermediate and Advanced, your goal will be to hit it within the gate.)

To view these drills in action and get some additional ideas on how to add spacing, variability, and challenge to your "training to learn" practice, visit – https://youtu.be/Hi2TRXFWVPM

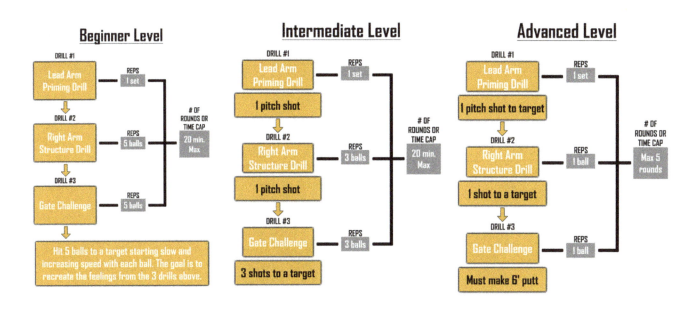

Golf Practice | 31

Practice Circuit 7 – Compression Master

The Goal

To help you make consistently solid and stable iron shots by helping you improve the compression in your swing.

What to do

Drill 1 – dynamic posture priming drill
No golf club is needed for this drill.

Take your stance and rotate your arms so that the palms of your hands are facing away from you.

Rotate into your backswing until your lead hand is in line with your trailing leg.

From here, begin to rotate back towards impact and, as you make this move, push your butt (or, as GLT's English coaching contingent would say: 'arse') back as if you were pushing up against a wall.

As you rotate towards impact stop as your hands return to the original position – you should be able to feel a majority of your weight is on your front foot.

Complete 5 reps before hitting a golf ball.

Drill 2 – Divot Ladder Drill

Use face spray or a golf tee to make a point of reference on the ground. You will make 3 swings during this drill.

For swing 1 you must make a divot as close to the line as possible.

Swing 2 must then start exactly where the divot where the previous divot finished.

Swing 3 must start where divot 2 ended.

Complete all three successfully before hitting a shot.

Drill 3 – Club Drag Drill

Take your normal set up and place the club head 2 ft behind your trail foot and in line with the ball of your foot.

Apply slight pressure to the club handle by pushing down.

Start to rotate your body so that the club drags along the ground, all the while maintaining the slight pressure.

Complete 3 reps before hitting a golf ball.

To view these drills in action and get some additional ideas on how to add spacing, variability, and challenge to your "training to learn" practice, visit – https://youtu.be/kJ-XXM5aYEI

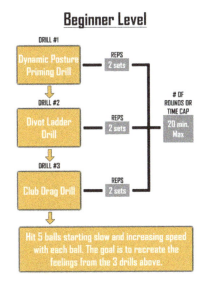
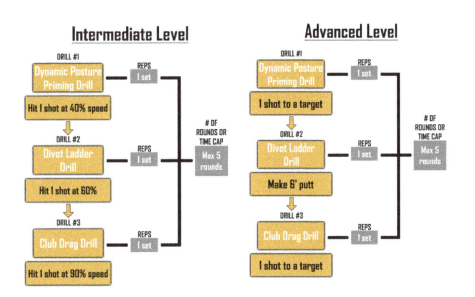

Golf Practice | 33

Practice Circuit 8 – Quality Of Strike

The Goal

Use these 3 drills to improve club face stability through the strike and well as club delivery into impact and overall body movement. Each drill is designed to help you self-discover what these core components of quality ball striking feel like.

What to Do

Drill 1 – alignment rod rotation
For this drill you will need an alignment rod and a 7 iron.

Place the alignment rod halfway down the club and then grip it as normal.

Take your normal 7 iron set up and make a backswing until your lead arm is parallel to the ground.

Then make a down swing motion where you rotate through impact – without the alignment rod hitting you.

Make 2 successful practice reps and then complete 1 rep with a ball (at no more than 70% of your swing speed).

Drill 2 – Step Through Drill
Take your 7 iron and adopt your usual stance for this club.

Then take your lead leg and put your feet together.

Make a full swing and, as you start the down swing, step the lead foot forward towards the target (and therefore back to its original starting position).

Make 2 successful practice reps and then hit 1 golf ball performing the drill.

Drill 3 – Through The Ball Move

Take your 7 iron and hold it horizontally to the ground, allowing it to simply hang at your knees.

Holding the club head in the lead hand, rotate to the top of the backswing keeping your hands in the same position.

Then, as you begin the downswing rotation, imagine you're trying to pull the head of the club off (an action which allows your lower body to move left and upper body to rotate).

Do one rep of this drill and then hit 1 ball trying to feel the same movement.
To view these drills in action and get some additional ideas on how to add spacing, variability, and challenge to your "training to learn" practice, visit - https://youtu.be/cB08w-48dTo

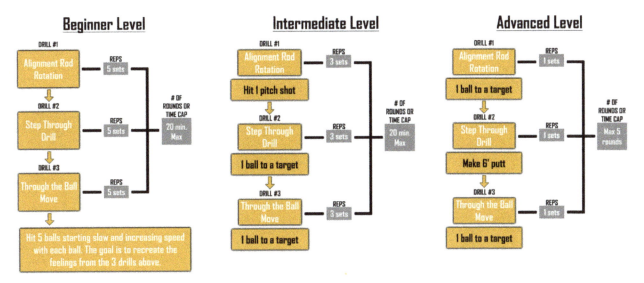

Golf Practice | 35

Practice Circuit 9 – Tour Wedge Sauce

The Goal

Time to debunk some pitching myths!

Through this challenge, not only will you start to conceptualize what needs to occur when it comes to the golf ball launch conditions, but you will also discover how to create the fundamentals of good wedge play.

What to Do

Drill 1 – Launch Drill
Place 2 alignment rods about 4ft apart and approximately 6ft in front of where you will be hitting the ball from.

Tie some string across the top, 3 ½ft above the ground to create something that looks a little like a goal.

The challenge now is to work out how you can hit your most lofted club through the goal… with a ¾ swing.

(If set up correctly, this will encourage you to launch your wedges between the range of 28-30 degrees which is the magic number when it comes to maximizing spin and increasing control.)

Drill 2 – no look shot
Make a pitch-shot length backswing and, before you begin the down swing, start to turn your head towards the target. This will encourage rotation and help you be more successful with drill 1.

Drill 3 – lead arm only

Take your normal pitching set up.

Take your trail arm off the club (right hand for right handed golfers) and try to hit a pitch shot.

The goal is primarily to make contact, followed by striking the ball with the center of the face.

(When we remove the trail arm, it encourages proper club deliver and body rotation, allowing the mass of the club to do the work for us.)

To view these drills in action and get some additional ideas on how to add spacing, variability, and challenge to your "training to learn" practice, visit - https://youtu.be/esedd5TgWDM

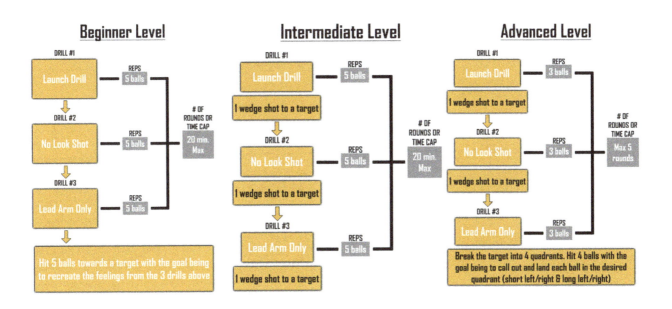

Golf Practice | 37

Practice Circuit 10 – Chipping

The Goal

Becoming better around the greens is vital to not only becoming better at golf, but to enjoying it more.

When you become more comfortable with your short game, it can free up your iron play as you no longer fear missing the green.

With these key concepts and drills, you will develop a better conceptual understanding of what goes into becoming a better chipper of the golf ball – and take that confidence out onto the course.

What to Do

Drill 1 – Lead Leg Only Drill
Take your normal chipping set up but place the ball forward, closer to your lead foot.

Lift your trailing foot off the ground and make a chipping motion, focusing on holding your finish without allowing your trail foot to touch the ground. You should also be making contact with the ground in the desired location.

Make one successful practice swing and then attempt to hit a ball doing the same, keeping the trail leg off the floor and holding your finish.

Drill 2 – Control The Arc
You will need 2 coins for this drill.

Place coin 1 half an inch behind the ball and coin 2 half an inch in front of the ball.

Hit a chip shot attempting to make contact with both coins as you hit the ball.

If this is done correctly both coins should go flying in the air and the strike on the golf ball should be solid.

(This will help you gain awareness of what the proper low point and ground contact should feel like. And, when done correctly, you can say goodbye to the thin and chunked chips!)

Drill 3 – Goldilocks Landing Zones

Place a towel on the chipping green where you think the ball needs to land to finish near the hole.

Ball 1 has to land past the towel, ball 2 has to land short of the towel and ball 3 has to land on the towel.

(This will help you calculate flight and distance, as well as build a better understanding of where the correct landing zone should be.)

To view these drills in action and get some additional ideas on how to add spacing, variability, and challenge to your "training to learn" practice, visit - https://youtu.be/Sfyjnwr_47g

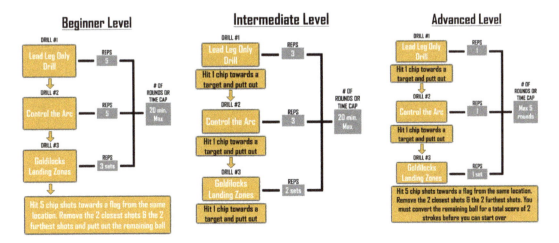

Golf Practice | 39

Practice Circuit 11 – Hole More Putts

The Goal

However simple putting may theoretically appear, it is one of the most over-complicated areas of the game. Through these drills, we'll help you self-discover strategies to free yourself of the complexities and anxieties of putting.

What to Do

Drill 1 – Coin Putting
You will need two coins for this drill.

Read the putt as normal and then place 1 coin where you want the ball to start, then place the second coin where you think the ball will enter into the hole.

Visualize the ball rolling over coin 1 and then coin 2 and then hit the putt.

After you have hit the putt, adjust the coins however you may need to, but hit no more than 5 attempts from any given location.

Drill 2 – Fringe Putting
Select a target on the opposite fringe of the green.

Hit 1 putt from between 25-50ft.

As soon as you hit the putt, say out loud if you think the ball will finish long, short or on target.

(The goal is to learn to couple your anticipated feedback with the actual outcome of the putt.)

Drill 3 – Putting Posture

Take your putter and hold it in front of you with your arms completely outstretched and parallel to the floor.

From here you will keep the putter parallel to the ground but bring your elbows into your side until they gently touch your ribcage.

From this position, maintain the arm structure you have just created while bending at the waist until the putter lies flat on the ground (feel free to flex your knees if it's more comfortable).

This will create what many consider a 'neutral' posture. Go through this process twice and then hit 1 putt.

To view these drills in action and get some additional ideas on how to add spacing, variability, and challenge to your "training to learn" practice, visit - https://youtu.be/mUVt8g3Gm7I

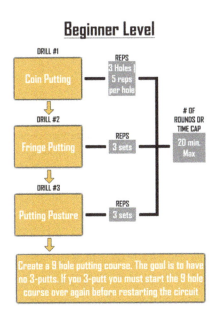

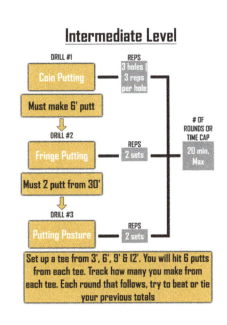

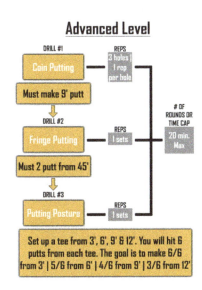

Golf Practice | 41

Practice Circuit 12 – Indoor Training 1

The Goal

The circuit will make it easier for you to create an indoor training environment that can actually help you change your swing.

What to Do

Drill 1 – Back Swing Chair Pivot

You will need a chair (or you can use your golf bag for this drill).

Position the chair so the seatback is almost touching your trail thigh (as close to the hip as possible).

The goal is to make practice swings where you pivot in the backswing and avoid hitting the chair.

(If you struggle with too much lateral slide or sway in the backswing, this drill will help you load more effectively – setting you up for success in the downswing.)

Drill 2 – Superflex Band Width Drill

You will need some sort of resistance band (we use a band from a company called SuperFlex).

Take your resistant band and place it under your lead foot, then take your grip with the band running through your fingers.

You will want the band to have a little slack in it as you address the ball.

From here you will make backswings focusing on stretching the band and maintaining width. Do not let the band win!

(This will help create more rotation of the torso, as well as help the club stay shallow in transition.)

Drill 3 – Medicine Ball Throws

For this drill you will ideally want a medicine ball, but a basketball or soccer ball with work as a stand-in.

Find a wall, and take your address position with the wall being your target.

The goal is to throw the ball at the wall towards a specific point (about 8ft high), making small backswings (with your lead arm parallel to the ground and finishing firmly on your lead side).

(This drill will help you load better into your trial side as well as sync up the rotation of the body and arms through impact and the release.)

To view these drills in action and get some additional ideas on how to add spacing, variability, and challenge to your "training to learn" practice, visit - https://youtu.be/LH2SM94jfAw

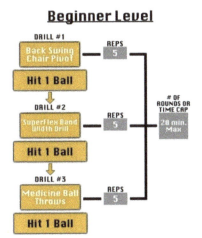 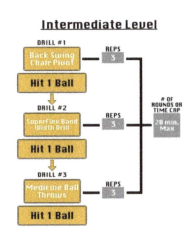 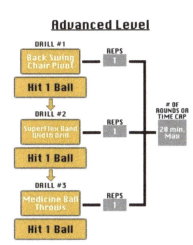

Golf Practice | 43

Practice Circuit 13 – Indoor Training 2

The Goal

This series of drills are for golfers that already have their own swing drills. Incorporating these 3 indoor drills into your training will not only help you retain the desired changes, but will also increase awareness and engagement in the finer details of your movements.

What to Do

Drill 1 – Slow Motion Swings
The goal here is to make a practice swing that lasts 30 seconds.

(This will help create more awareness of the desired movements as well as increase your understanding of the muscles being fired throughout your swing. You will be surprised how hard it is to move the club how you desire at such a slow pace.)

Drill 2 – Kinesthetic Motor Imagery
This is a crazy one, but there is strong scientific support for its effectiveness. Honestly.

You need no club for this drill.

Stand still and try to feel your entire golf swing without physically moving your body.

See if you can feel the muscles activate throughout the swing as you would if you were actually hitting a golf ball.

See if you can feel it at slow speeds as well as real time.

44 | Game Like Training

Drill 3 – Think Aloud

You will talk your entire routine aloud for this station. There are two goals here:

Allow you to spot any variance or mistakes within your routine – does it seem to change from swing to swing?

Help you to increase awareness of what you should focus on in your routine when out on the golf course.

To view these drills in action and get some additional ideas on how to add spacing, variability, and challenge to your "training to learn" practice, visit - https://youtu.be/Cluo3b5BQDc

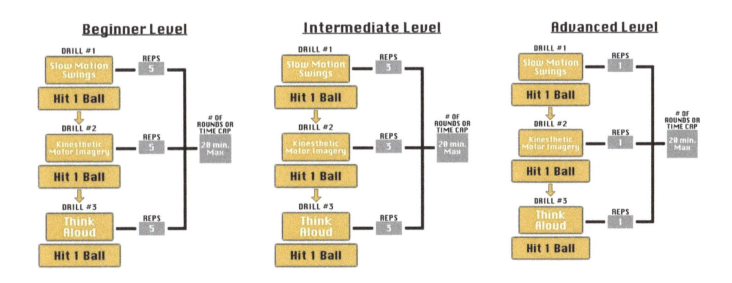

Golf Practice | 45

4 – Golf Practice
Training to Perform

Let's say you decided to become an Olympic swimmer. And let's also say that, on making this dramatic life decision, you were presented with the following options, which would you choose? Swim daily in your bath tub and perfect your stroke.

Go to the pool and learn to race against other swimmers.

Unless you happen to own the world's most impressive bath, the choice is clear. However, when it comes to golf, most players who restrict their development environment to the range, are effectively perfecting their competitive freestyle alongside their rubber ducky.

Now, if achieving a flawless swing is all that matters to you, there isn't necessarily a big problem with this. However, if you want to actually play great golf, you need to make sure you have (wait for it) the spacing, variability and challenge that enables contextual practice. Contextual practice is a pre-requisite to enabling a golfer to adapt to the environmental and psychological demands of the game.

In other words, a perfectly formed swing is irrelevant if you don't have the awareness to adapt your near-perfect Adam Scott impression to the environmental demands of the golf course – and deal with the mental tests that accompany a score card and pencil.

How does a golfer, shackled to the range, access those perfect swing mechanics on a lie that isn't flat? All these players have ever known is tackling artificially flat lies with their favorite club. How can they begin to adapt to even the slightest variation from that?

The simple answer is they can't. You are a range hitter, not a golfer. You are the bath tub backstroker, but you will never get a sniff of a medal.

We, as a sport, need to stop viewing the range as our training Mecca and start to see it as something very, very different – our Uber.

Uber didn't reinvent the landscape of urban travel because it sold us the idea of transport – ever since there were wheels, there was transport. Instead, it sold us the commodity we crave more than any other – time. It's fast, it's easy, it's always available, it's convenient – it is the golf range.

Golf Practice | 47

Remember Elon's Advice

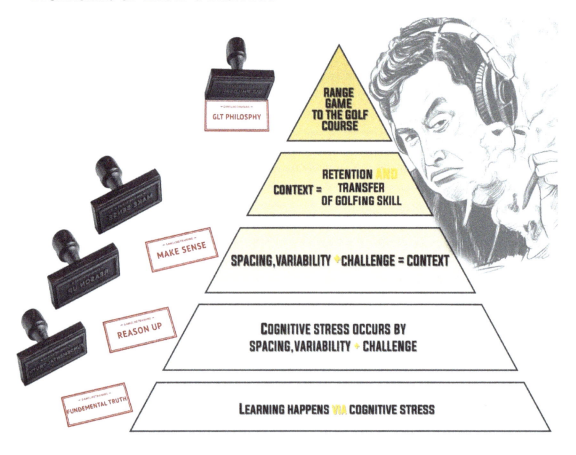

We know we're talking about Elon Musk a lot, but he seems like a man who rather likes being talked about, so we'll keep going. Let's remind ourselves of the Musk law of fundamental truth.

Our Fundamental Truth… Cognitive Stress Equals Learning

Hitting ball after ball, with the same target, same club and same mechanical approach does not create that cognitive stress. The best we can say is that it's giving yourself a (not terribly taxing) physical workout.

Reasoning Up… Spacing, Variability And Challenge

These are the three key elements for creating a state of cognitive stress – adding the all-important **context** to your practice. On the course, you'll never hit 10 shots in a row to the same target with the same club. You'll never even hit two because the nature of the game dictates that every shot is a different problem from the last. That's why the interleaved practice we discussed earlier is the way to achieve meaningful practice and retain learnings from the range. Learning and performing however, should never be mistaken for the same thing.

This makes sense because… we have developed strategies that we're sharing in this book that are proven to help you practice in a more deliberate and effective way and retain what you learn – even if you're on the range.

So, now we've recapped our core principles on learning, the focus of this book is going to be much more about how we **transfer** those learnings onto the golf course and perform.

To maximize this state of transfer a golfer's practice needs to **recreate** and **simulate** specific situations they will face on the golf course. This will allow you to **regulate** your practice and help you master a vitally important piece of psychological processing – **chunking.**

Uptown Chunk

It doesn't matter if you're a beginner, intermediate or advanced golfer, recreating and simulating the specific challenges you will face on the golf course is such a powerful training methodology for one main reason – it gives you the opportunity to chunk. Which isn't as terrible as it sounds.

Imagine a piece of information. Within that piece of information there are details, nuances, concepts, movements and much more. The piece of information is what's being referred to as a chunk and is stored in our memory. Chunks then become accessible pieces of information that, if trained to do so, golfers can retrieve and use in a tournament situation.

To be accessible during the competition, your practice must heavily involve both the recreation and the simulation of game-like situations.

Over a period of time the stimulus that is created from the environment around a golfer will fire the right patterns, connect to the right chunks of information and allow you to transfer skills you've practiced into tournament play.

It's this interaction between the brain, body and the environment that must happen for golfers to a.) acquire new skills and b.) transfer them into competition, or as some like to say, take their range game to the course.

Golf: A Novel

This is a great visual to help you decipher what we've just talked about, and link it to sporting performance.

Think about how the alphabet acts as the building blocks for a novel. On their own, individual letters mean nothing. But even the simplest organization allows them to form words, which have meaning. Then further organization leads to the formation of sentences, sentences evolve into paragraphs and paragraphs into chapters, culminating in a novel (which, may or may not be about golf).

The golf shot works the same way. Just hitting a ball down a golf range is comparable to the individual letters on a page, it really has no context.

But when we add, say, a target, affordances for the wind and perhaps giving the shot a score out of 10 we begin to create a meaning – although our finished novel remains a long way off.

To reach that completeness of narrative, we need differing lies, slopes, stances – the sort of demands that every golfer must be exposed to in order to create clear mental representations of a challenge.

Time and again the ability to quickly and efficiently process information that is specific to a performance environment has been hailed as a key component of elite sports performance – creating undeniable connections between motor skills and information processing activities.

And what we want to create is a chunking process that has evolved sufficiently to help golfers transfer skills onto the course.

This doesn't mean you may only go and practice on the course – we've already acknowledged that the most precious commodity in our world right now is time. But, with exercises in this book that use interleaved practice strategies to make range practice more rewarding, we're more interested in changing the 'how' of your practice than necessarily the 'where'.

Admittedly though, the strategies we are about to share – built around **game like practice** and **constraints led learning** – are designed for a highly motivated golfer with a little more time on their hands, access to a practice facility that has a designated chipping area… or perhaps that lucky devil who lives on a golf course and can sneak out at dusk for an hour when the kids are in bed.

We would encourage, however, that anyone from pros, to amateurs competing in ranked events, to juniors and collegiate golfers with ambitions to go pro (anyone whose main aim is to play better tournament golf), to try and make your practice as contextual as you possibly can – which means, however you're able to do it, creating the contextual inferences you'll encounter on the course.

Researchers would call this the ecological approach to learning. At Game Like Training we don't believe this to be the only way, but we do see it as an important part of the **learning continuum**, a method that is proven to induce deeper learning and help you 'train to perform' and more effectively transfer your learnt skills onto the course.

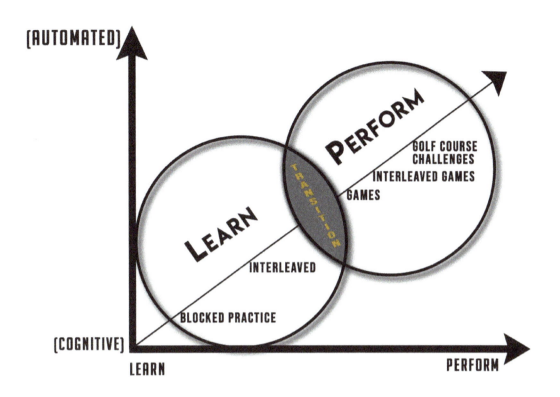

This fancy chart represents what we discussed in the Training to Learn chapter. You can see that blocked practice and interleaved practice fall into the learning phase of the continuum. Deliberate engagement in the Training to Learn circuits that we shared earlier are key to helping you retain the movement skills you're trying to master.

Golf Practice | 53

The Things That Tiger Signs

The tasks that we are about to share with you are the start of the process of training to perform and becoming a more **automated** golfer. Let's use a Tiger Woods analogy to get you in the right frame of mind for training to perform (don't worry, it's not a dirty one).

In 1996, Tiger Woods signed a preposterously lucrative sponsorship deal with Nike. As he put pen to paper and wrote his signature, his body was enabled by what is known as a **generalized motor pattern**. Motor programs allow the brain and body to connect and produce a coordinated set of movements (as you already know from our Training to Learn chapter) involving both voluntary and reflex actions, like signing your name.

Now imagine if the paper that Tiger signed his name on was replaced by a chalk board or a sand pit (unlikely we know) but these scenarios would result in Tiger having to adapt his generalized motor pattern that he has created over the years, to the different conditions of chalk and sand.

Over the years (even pre-1996,) it is likely that Tiger has signed his name thousands of times and had an extremely effective generalized motor pattern for this activity, making it easier for him to adapt.

Previous signings on brims of hats, golf balls, head covers, napkins in bars and other uneven surfaces that it's best not to think about, would also give him a data bank of past experiences to which he could refer, making the success of crossing the 'T' and dotting the 'I' a simple task.

Tiger's golf is no different. Over the years, he has hit thousands and thousands of balls and developed a highly effective generalized motor pattern. He has also played on hundreds of different courses, in almost every condition imaginable, enabling him to 'chunk' information and therefore learn to adapt his generalized motor pattern.

Basically, Tiger's vast experience allows him to adapt his swing to almost any situation – not because he's spent all that time mastering his technique, but because he spent it experiencing, learning and retaining an encyclopedia of tournament scenarios.

Turn On The Motor

Hopefully, at this stage of the book, you're starting to see that evolving a motor program for your golf swing is going to take…

Repetition…

of the total process of hitting a shot…

driven by contextual practice…

Of course, the goal of practice is not to develop the perfect repeatable swing, it is to develop a generalized motor program (your swing) that you then must learn to adapt to the environmental demands of the golf course.

Golf is, after all, a problem-solving task in which the problem involves sending the ball from point A toward point B.

The solution to the problem involves a *process* that requires situational awareness, perception, movement planning, retrieving a motor program and adapting the motor program from memory – all before the swing is executed.

During competitive play a golfer has to do all of this while adapting to the demands of the environment (the wind or an uneven lie being prime examples) not to mention the stresses contributed by the competition and its outcomes. And these stresses are all relative, whether it's a putt for your first major victory, tour card or the lowest net score in the Sunday medal, that stress response is still going to fire.

The coming chapter, you'll be pleased to hear, is going to take all of this knowledge and theory we just shared and turn it into something you can do.

Now, in addition to the spacing, variability and challenge that you learned in the first chapters, we're going to begin to establish your chunking process through recreation and simulation – ultimately helping you adapt your generalized motor pattern to the demands of the golf course and outcome pressures. You're going to love it. Seriously

5 – Golf Practice
Training to Perform: Practical Application

Performance Games

Experts in motor learning, cognition and sports science, as well as leading golf coaches, all say recreating and simulating specific situations a golfer will face on the course directly influence the development of 'chunks' – and therefore the development of the corresponding skills.

What we are about to share are specifically designed tasks called 'performance games' that relate to different areas of your game.

Players at a level closer to beginner may decide to try a single performance game at any one time, such as a putting game, while more advanced golfers may decide to interleave 2 games, for example…

> Hit 5 shots from a full swing game…
> …and then 5 putts from a putting game…
> …before returning back to the full swing game…
> …and repeat!

The most advanced players may want to select multiple performance games, hitting one shot from game A, one shot from game B, one shot from game C and one shot from game D and then repeating this process until all selected games are complete.

Speed Putting
Distance dominator

Game
Improving Distance Control

Goal
The goal is to hit as many putts away from yourself – and then towards yourself – as possible.

Rules
When hitting away, each ball is to roll further than the previous ball. This continues until the set boundary at the other side has been reached or crossed. An alignment rod or a row of tees would make a great boundary.

When reached or crossed, leave the last golf ball you hit before the line was crossed and collect all the other golf balls.

Now hit putts working back to yourself. Each following putt should come up short of the previous putt.

Do this until you have no more room to putt.

Scoring system
25 feet: Level 1 = 12 putts away/ 12 putts towards
25 feet: Level 2 = 17 putts away/ 17 putts towards
35 feet: Level 1 = 17 putts away/ 17 putts towards
35 feet: Level 2 = 25 putts away/ 25 putts towards

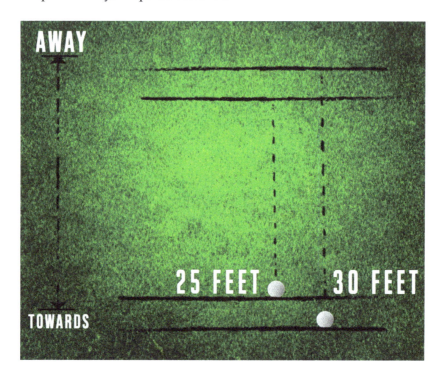

Lag Putting
Zone to zone

Game
Developing distance control and lag putting by getting you to hit golf balls to each of the circled zones.

Goal
Accumulate as many points as possible. Starting in 1 of the 4 circles, you have 3 golf balls, leaving the other 3 circles open. The aim is to get 1 golf ball in each of those open circles.

Rules
Games must be recorded every time.

Scoring system
Level 1: In circle = 10 points, long = 0 points, short = 0 points
Level 2: In circle = 10 points, long = 0 points, short = -5 points
Level 3: In circle = 10 points, long = -5 points, short -10 points

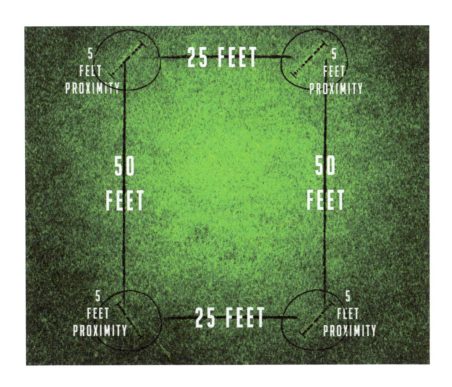

Golf Practice | 59

Hole-Out Putting
PGA Tour putt

Game
To improve your hole-out ability inside 15 feet.

Goal
Hole as many putts as possible from each distance tee.

Rules
Place a total of 24 tees in the ground. 6 tees in the ground at 3 ft from the hole, 6 tees at 6 ft from the hole, 6 tees at 9ft from the hole and 6 tees at 12 ft from the hole (see diagram below).
A player only gets 1 attempt per tee, this provides a 24 total putts.
If you start the game, you must complete it.

Scoring system
Every putt holed is worth 1 point.
Level 1: 4/6 from 3 feet, 3/6 from 6 feet, 2/6 from 9 feet, 1/6 from 12 feet.
Level 2: 5/6 from 3 feet, 4/6 from 6 feet, 4/6 from 9 feet, 2/6 from 12 feet.
Level 3: 6/6 from 3 feet, 5/6 from 6 feet, 4/6 from 9 feet, 3/6 from 12 feet.
Level 4: 6/6 from 3 feet, 6/6 from 6 feet, 5/6 from 9 feet, 4/6 from 12 feet.

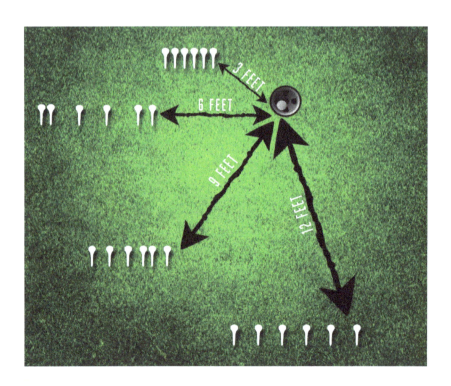

Putting Challenge
Putting cup

Game
Working on competitive play – using both distance & direction – you will play 9 holes on the putting green.

Goal
Complete the course set up in as few strokes as possible while scoring as many points as possible. Coaches can dictate the difficulty of the course based on the player's performance.

Rules
Only one golf ball is to be used, and scores must be recorded every time.
The length of the putt must also be recorded on scorecard.

Scoring system
Level 1: 4putt = 0 pts, 3putt = 10 pts, 2putt = 20 pts, 1putt = 30 pts
Level 2: 3putt = 0 pts, 2putt = 10 pts, 1putt = 20 pts, 4putt = -10 pts
Level 3: 2putt = 0 pts, 1putt = 10 pts, 3putt = -10 pts, 4putt = -20 pts

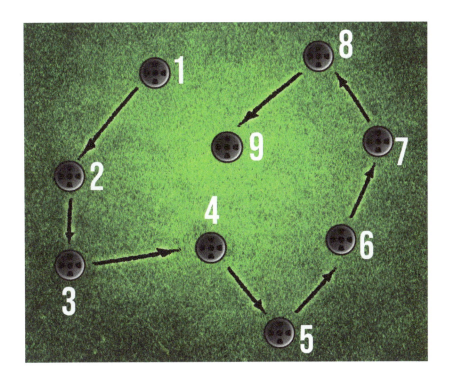

Putting Challenge
2-2-1 putting

Game
Building further on your lag putting and ability to hole-out under stress.

Goal
Successfully 2-putt twice from distance and then hole a short range putt under pressure.

Rules
This game is a completion task.
All '2 putt' holes will range from 20-60 feet and all '1 putt' holes will range from 6-12 feet.
Select a putt ranging from 20-60 feet based on your ability level and attempt to 2-putt. If you fail, start the game again. If you are successful select a different 20-60 ft putt and attempt to 2-putt. If you're successful you can move on to the final short putt... but if you fail to 2-putt, you must restart the game from the beginning.
Repeat the above process with the final short putt.
(Oh, and if you have to restart the game it's best not to hit the exact same putts you did in the previous attempt.)

Scoring system
Level 1: If at any point you do not make a par (2 putts for the long putts and 1 putt for the short putt) on the hole, you must start the game over at hole #1. You have 1 hour to complete.
Level 2: Bring back all second putts one putter length, if you do not make a par on the hole, you must start the game over again at hole #1. You have 1 hour to complete.

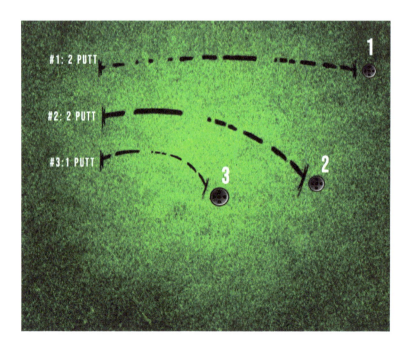

Short Game – Chipping And Putting
Par 18 chipping

Game
A chipping game with more variability due to the length of grass surrounding the ball.

Goal
Get up and down in as few shots as possible.

Rules
Pick 9 different locations around the green. Mark the locations with a tee or a cone as shown in the diagram below.
Only 1 golf ball is to be played at the 9 different locations around the green.
You must chip the ball as close as you can to the hole and hole out with a putter.

Scoring system
Keep your score relative to par, (every hole is a par 2) OR use the advanced points system detailed below and attempt to progress through the levels.
Level 1: 1 chip, 3 putts = 0 points. 1 chip, 2 putts = 10 points. 1 chip, 1 putt = 20 points.
Level 2: 1 chip, 3 putts = -5 points. 1 chip, 2 putts = 0 points, 1 chip, 1 putt = 10 points. 1 chip, 0 putts = 20 points.
Level 3: 1 chip, 3 putts = -10 points. 1 chip, 2 putts = -5 points. 1 chip, 1 putt = 0 points. 1 chip, 0 putts 10 points

Golf Practice | 63

Short Game – Bunker Play
Pick and mix

Game
Creating constant change to develop adaptability skills. This game incorporates different slope types with different distances and different targets… with only 1 attempt to get it right!

Goal
Hit balls from each station in the bunker into any pre-selected basket.

Rules
Using the diagram above set the baskets out on the green and set station markers in the bunker. When setting station markers in the bunker be sure to have one uphill, flat and downhill lie.
Then place 1 golf ball per station.
You must select your target basket prior to hitting the shot and measure the distance.

Scoring system
Level 1: Basket hit = 5 points, Basket holed = 10 points, Basket missed = 0 points
Level 2: Basket hit = 0 points, Basket holed = 10 points, Basket missed = -5 points
Level 3: Basket hit = 0 points, Basket holed = 5 points, Basket missed = -10 points

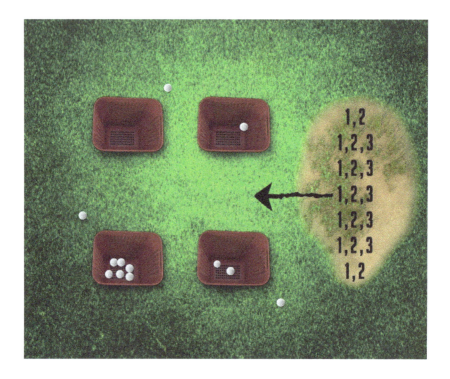

Short Game – Pitching
Finesse wedges

Game
Find out how your wedge work, from 10-40 yards, compares to players on the PGA Tour.

Goal
To hit the ball as close to the hole as possible from 10-40 yards.

Rules
Select 20 different locations to hit a pitch shot from.
Go through your whole process on each shot and execute.
Walk to the green and measure the proximity your ball finished from the target and award yourself the relevant amount of points.
Repeat this process until all balls are hit and you can compare your score to the PGA Tour average

Scoring system
Hole out: 5 points
Inside 3 feet: 3 points
Inside 6 feet: 1 point
Inside 9 feet: 0 point
Miss the green: -1 point

Level 1 = 14 points
Level 2 = 18 points
Level 3 = 22 +
A PGA Tour golfer would consistently be scoring 20+ points

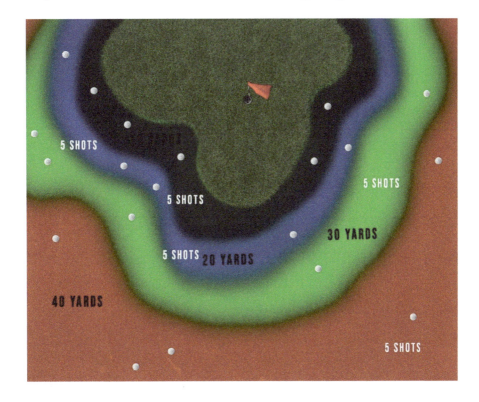

Golf Practice | 65

Full Swing – Tee Shots
Down the line

Game
This game will help you develop confidence and driving accuracy from the tee.

Goal
To hit each tee shot inside the required 'dispersion area'.

Rules
Pick an area on the golf range that represents an imaginary fairway. This will be your dispersion area.
Only one attempt per dispersion area is allowed.
Once you have attempted to hit that dispersion area create a new imaginary fairway and repeat.
Points are to be recorded every time.

Scoring system
Level 1:
Dispersion area hit = 10 points
Dispersion area miss = 0 points
Level 2:
Dispersion area hit = 10 points
Dispersion area miss = -5 points

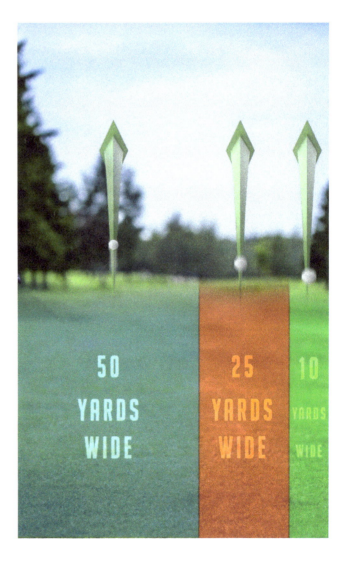

Full Swing – Shot Shaping
Tiger's 9

Game
Tiger's 9 involves hitting all 9 shots in golf – straight, draw and fade with each shot to be hit at a low, medium and high height.

Goal
Execute every shot in succession.

Rules
You aren't allowed to attempt the same shot twice.
Scores must be recorded every time.

Scoring system
Level 1:
Shot hit well as intended = 10 points
Shot hit poorly but in play = 5 points
Shot hit poorly, cost or penalty = 0 points
Level 2:
Shot hit well as intended = 10 points
Shot hit poorly but in play = 0 points
Shot hit poorly, cost or penalty = -5 points

Golf Practice | 67

Full Swing – Approach Shots
Numbers game

Game
This game will help you pick more specific targets when shooting at a green on the golf course.

Goal
Hit the designated part of the green.

Rules
Divide the green up into four quadrants.
Depending on the level you select to play hit a golf ball at the selected quadrant.
If successful move on to the next quadrant keeping track of the total number of balls you use.
Scores must be recorded each time the game is played to track progress or regression. The lower the number of balls it takes you to hit all 4 quadrants the better.

Scoring system
Level 1 - In as few balls as possible, hit quadrant 1, 2, 3 and 4 from the distance you desire to practice.
Level 2 – In as few balls as possible, hit quadrant 1, 2, 3 and 4 but you can never shoot at the same quadrant with successive shots.
Level 3 – Play level 2 but have 2 greens divided up into 4 quadrants, alternate attempts between greens. Never hit at the same green or the same quadrant in succession until it's the final quadrant on the final green.

Interleaving Of Performance Games

As we mentioned at the beginning of this chapter, interleaving of performance games is a great way to increase spacing, variability and challenge – and, therefore, make you better at golf. And we mean real golf in real tournaments, on a real course, with real grass (you get the idea).

Interleaving the games encourages chaos, stress and emotion whereas only ever engaging in a standalone performance game reduces the likelihood of effective skill transfer from practice onto the course (although, this is clearly an acceptable way to begin your journey if you're a novice golfer).

However, it would be GLT's recommendation that the more accomplished player interleaves performance games, therefore enhancing the chance of skill transfer to the golf course.

For example, take Par 18 Chipping (page 63). Attempting to make 9 up-and-downs in a row would never happen on the course, but if we add in Tiger's 9 (page 67) and 2-2-1 Putting (page 62) and interleave these games we now get closer to the real game of golf – basically by increasing the spacing, variability and challenge we experience and ultimately adding game-like context.

And, if you need a bit more support or structure for interleaving the games, here's the GLT template to help.

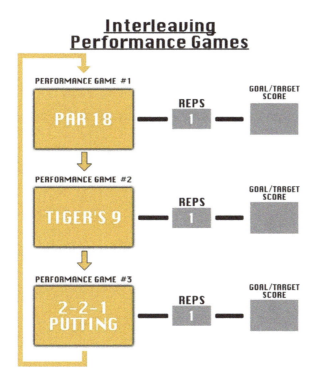

Download the above template at https://www.gltgolf.com/golf-coach-instructor-resource.html

Golf Practice | 69

Interleaving performance games with training to learn circuits

There is even a time when we should be interleaving our training to learn tasks with the performance games. This is known as the **Transition Phase** and is the point when you are now training to perform by preparing yourself for the environmental and psychological demands of the golf course.

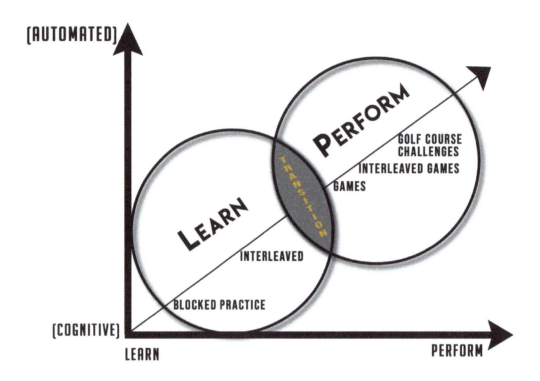

The Transition Phase, represented by the grey area on the diagram, is the stage of your practice where you begin to retain the desired swing movements and now need to test these movements in a more contextual environment – ensuring your learned skills will begin to transfer effectively to the course and eventually into competition.

So, when you feel you're at the Transition Phase, this GLT template can help you successfully interleave training to learn tasks that will help you learn and retain golf swing movements alongside performance games that will help you successfully transfer those skills onto the course.

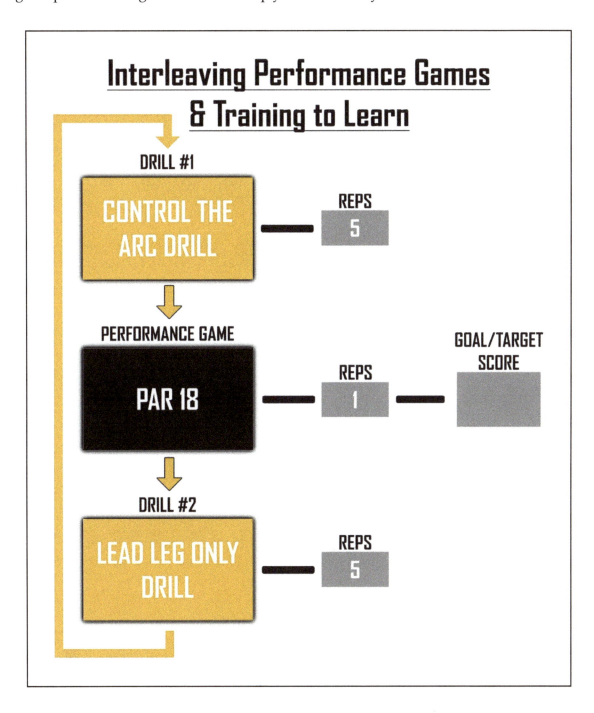

Control the arc drill – Practice circuit 10, pages 38-39
Par 18 chipping – Training to perform, page 63
Lead leg only drill – Practice circuit 10, page 38

On course golf practice

The final piece of the learning performance continuum – or, more simply, the point when we finally hit the golf course – is when we actually try to make golf harder than anything we will face in a tournament. At this point we are trying to maximize your level of skill-transfer and are fully immersed in the training to perform world.
So far, our journey should look a little like this…

We've improved our swing motion AND done it in a way where the changes we've made are more likely to be retained over time (thanks to our interleaved circuits).

We've begun to transition towards a more performance-orientated approach to practice – as our practice circuits began to incorporate performance games.

We've created the optimal amount of spacing, variability and challenge in more performance based circuits, helping us recreate and simulate situations we'll face on the course

We know how to adapt our movement patterns to the environment of the course, as well as beginning to develop chunks that allow us to practice and learn the total process of every shot and scenario.

Which is admittedly an awful lot to have achieved in 100 or so pages. But at some point, this total process of learning has to be tested… under stress.

Out on the course, or particularly in a competition, it is highly likely that a golfer's **stress response** will be triggered at some point. Therefore, it makes sense that all golfers should practice their retained movement skills in a way that tests them under stress, basically inoculating them against the adverse effects of performing under pressure.

This stress response happens in 4 stages:

The **environmental demand** of the golf shot. This could be the physical ability to hit the shot or the psychology behind the shot. Clearing a large amount of water is a good example.

Then comes the **perception of the environmental demand**. How much physical or psychological threat does the shot contain. 220 yards to an island green is more than a 100-yard shot where only the first 50 needs to be covered by water.

Based on this perception, the golfer experiences a **stress response**, that takes both a physical and psychological form – e.g. arousal, muscle tension and shifts in focus.

Finally, at this stage, there is a **consequence,** usually manifesting as a poor golf swing.

In short, as these 4 stages unfold, it becomes harder and harder to access your best motor pattern (golf swing) in the face of all this arousal, tension and loss of focus.

Therefore, golfers who truly want to play to their full potential must experience and manage this stress response in practice if they are going to master the art of flow in competition.

At GLT, we have a way to make this happened. Constraint-led learning challenges that take place (gasp) on the golf course.

This type of practice involves placing 'constraints' on either the learner, the task or the environment that will result in certain behaviours emerging from the player.

Successful completion of the task depends on the golfer developing situational awareness and actively discovering solutions for the problems created by the constraints.

This is the secret sauce to transferring golfing skills, not least because these challenges also encourage self-determination and intrinsic motivation – a couple of personal traits that no great golfer can do without.

Constraints-led learning – on course stress training challenges

2 Ball – Worst Ball

Game
To shoot as low a score as possible while playing from your worst ball after each shot.

Goal
This challenge will help you not only deal with adversity but will also help you develop strategies and awareness of how to execute quality golf shots when you need to.

Rules
From the tee, hit two shots. You will then select the worst positioned ball to be played for your next shot.
From this position, you will again hit two shots to the target. Again, select the worst of the two to be played for your third shot.
Repeat this until you are on the green.

Once on the putting green:

Intermediate level – will only play one ball once on the green, holing out as normal.
Advanced level – continue to play the worst ball on the green until both putts are made.
Tour level –same as advanced, but drawback each putt 3 feet until both putts are made.

Link: https://youtu.be/lVXiAeEMaWA

The Pressure Cooker

Game
A challenge where no area of your game is safe!

Goal
The goal is to increase the challenge level of the golf course, putting an emphasis on tee-shot accuracy, yet penalizing you for guiding the ball into play.

There is also an emphasis on approach-shot accuracy helping you develop better on-course strategies and processes.

Rules
Play your tee shot as normal
If you hit the fairway, play the next shot as normal.
If you miss the fairway, you must pull the ball back 10-30 yards (depending on skill level) leaving it in the rough to play the next shot
On your approach, if you hit the green, putt out as normal.
If you miss the green, you must complete the up and down or receive the following consequence:

Intermediate level – lose 1 life for failing to complete the up and down (unlimited lives)
Advanced – Same as intermediate but you only have 3 lives for 9 holes or 5 lives for 18 holes.
Tour level – any lost life results in a restart of that hole and players have 3 hours to complete nine holes.

(Make sure to keep track of all lives lost and scores so that you can set goals and track your progress over time.)

Link: https://youtu.be/l5xvrxl9MO0

Golf Practice | 75

The Eliminator

Game
It's one thing to have good course management… but being able to execute is a very different basket of balls altogether.

Goal
This challenge forces you to think a little more about course strategy as well as understanding how strategy and your tendencies go hand in hand.

Rules
From the tee, select a side of the hole you want to eliminate (left or right side of the fairway) and hit your tee shot.
If your tee ball lands in your eliminated area, it is a 2-stroke penalty. If you hit the correct side of the hole there is no penalty.
From this position, play the approach shot and select which side of the flag you are eliminating (left or right of the flag).
Again, any shot that lands in the eliminated are is a 2-stroke penalty and no penalty for hitting the correct side of the green.
After the approach shot is hit, finish the hole as normal and record your score under these constraints.

Link: https://youtu.be/fZ2lW5yLPcU

The Sharp Shooter

Game
Get ready to fire some birdies in competition through experiencing it in practice.

Goal
This game is designed to help you with outcome stress when using the driver and sharpen your scoring wedges

Rules
Hit the tee shot as normal with the goal of hitting the fairway.
From there, pick up your tee shot and move it to between 50-90 yards, keeping it in the same cut of grass as where your tee shot finished.
To earn an additional bonus ball for your approach shot, your drive must have:
Intermediate level – hit the fairway or within 1 club length of fairway
Advanced level – hit the fairway
Tour level – cut the fairway in half and hit the correct half
From 50-90 yards play your approach shot and the bonus ball if you earned it.
Select your best ball and play out.

Scoring system
Intermediate level: < +5 over
Advanced level: < even par
Tour level: < -5 under

Link: https://youtu.be/uVz5feNhAjU

Shot Shaper

Game
You can shape the ball on the range, but can you shape the ball when faced with the chaos of the golf course?

Goal
To challenge yourself to shape shots under stress and to adapt to the constraints of the performance environment (also known as the golf course).

Rules
Select a draw or fade to play for the entire nine holes.
Every time you hit the correct shape, subtract .5 (half a stroke) from your score.
Every time you do not hit the correct shape, add 1 full stroke to your score. (Shot shapes only apply to shots outside of 100 yards.)
Once you reach the green, putt out as normal and record your score.

Scoring system
For example…

Total strokes to hole out	= 4
Correct shape – tee shot	= -0.5
Incorrect shape – approach	= +1
Adjusted total score	= 4.5

Link: https://youtu.be/TzaNPN7hnBM

> 'But coach', we hear you whimper, 'the members (and my wife/husband/needy cat) will murder me if I try and play these games on the course'.

Fair point. Luckily though, there is a way to try out all of these challenges even if you're not willing the risk the wrath of the club or your partner (or cat).

As a wise man once (sort of) said: if you can't bring yourself to the course, bring the course to you'.

High-speed photography, computer analysis, launch monitors, bio-mechanics and sports science have been a catalyst for enormous improvement in the understanding of the swing – for golfers at every level.

These new methods have ushered in a flood of instructional material through books, magazines, videos and online courses on the golf swing (or, as we like to call it, training to learn practice).

Weirdly, there is nowhere near the same depth or breadth of resource to help you train for performance.

Probably the most well-known of these swing analysis resources is good old Trackman. (If you don't know what that is, essentially it's the little orange boxes you see all over PGA Tour practice ranges. They're like mini radars that measure the flight of your ball in order to analyze the effectiveness of your swing. Oh, and they probably cost more than your car.)

And, in fairness to Trackman, they have also produced a piece of software that focuses more on training to perform, called Trackman Combine.

What is the Trackman Combine?

The Trackman Combine is a test which enables players to hit a variety of shots, under game-like conditions on the range

Players begin by hitting three shots at a target 60 yards away, then repeat this at 70, 80, 90, 100, 120, 140, 160 and 180 yards.

Finally, three shots are hit with a driver. This 'round' is then repeated to give a total of 60 shots, each of which are scored from 0-100 by the Trackman system.

Every player who completes the Combine gets the following stats:

- A Combine score for each yardage
- An aggregate score for the 60 shot Combine
- A ranking within your handicap group for each yardage
- Average distance from the pin at each yardage
- Average driver distance and accuracy

Around the world, more than 10,000 golfers of all abilities have used the Trackman Combine, and it's easy to see the attraction.

You get immediate and definitive feedback about your performance with a variety of different clubs, while hitting shots under pressure.

It tells your right away where your game is weak or strong in relation to other golfers of similar ability. You can even take part in Combine competitions if you like.

But (and it's a pretty big but)

Let's start with drawback number one. You can only do it at a facility that has the Trackman technology.

More importantly, there's evidence that Trackman Combine is not the most effective way to practice, and even golfers who improve their Combine stats find it difficult to reproduce this improved shot-making on the golf course.

The reason for this can be found, surprisingly, in a popular athletic training regime which does seem to provide transferable benefits. It's called CrossFit.

What is CrossFit (and why does it work)

CrossFit is designed to develop all-round strength and conditioning through a variety of high intensity (i.e. vomit-inducingly hard) functional movements.

Participants undertake a Workout of the Day (WOD) incorporating a number of these movements, but the WODs are almost infinitely variable, with a different workout challenge offered every day (unlike the Combine which has just one version of its test).

A typical WOD is the so-called 'Fran' which involves sets of 21, 15 and 9 reps of barbell thrusters and pull-ups (and who doesn't love a pull-up).

A CrossFit participant that does a Fran during their Monday gym session will not do the same thing on the Tuesday. In fact they may not do this exact workout for months.

They will however be exposed to other workouts that contain these movements in the coming weeks (at this point of the book you will know where we are going with this – spacing, variability and challenge).

The interesting thing about CrossFit is that participants report that tackling different WODs seems to improve their performance in all exercises and workouts, not to mention improving performance in their chosen sport.

One main reason for this seems to be that, while all the exercises demand strength, mobility, co-ordination and balance, the differences between them also demand a considerable degree of mental application and concentration.

In other words, the ever-changing demands of the tasks are developing not only your movement but the way your brain responds to these movements.

But, while the benefits may be obvious for a super-ripped, high intensity athlete, what on earth has it got to offer for golfers?

The GLT answer

Through a training model like this, a golfer is placing certain contextual and cognitive demands on their practice session – something the Trackman Combine does not.

As we have said a very-nearly-boring amount of times in this book, at Game Like Training we help golfers of all levels improve their games by incorporating scientific principles of learning into their practice regimes.

We've done this so far by devising routines which include the essential elements of spacing, variability and challenge, and it occurs to us that these are also the aspects of CrossFit which have made it so successful.

So, if you can't get access to the golf course and take on our on-course stress challenges, bring the course to the range by creating your own 'golf workouts of the day' (or Golf WODs as a true Crosfitter might say).

We've created our own Golf WODs (like the one below), inspired by the environment of learning and skill-transference that CrossFit offers its athletes.

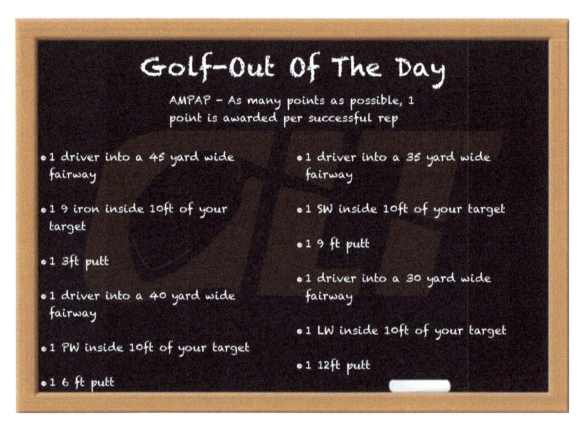

You can access more 'Golf-outs of the day' for free here:

https://www.youtube.com/playlist?list=PLtmCPzBk3iRMYyTVbfdprYpZhCt2jxXwG

Solutions like the Trackman Combine is undoubtedly a more effective way to practice that simply pinging balls into space for 45 minutes. But at the end of the day, it is still simply another standardized test that lacks the context, spacing, variability and challenge to help you take what you've learned onto the course.

But in CrossFit, the principle works as simply as this. Every day you train, thanks to the high spacing, variability, challenge and context in the WOD, you are becoming better at CrossFit.

Until something like the Trackman Combine can produce 365 different challenges, and serve up a different practice scenario every time you use it, all you are doing is improving your test scores, not your golf.

Ultimately, this is why when a CrossFit athlete competes their performance supersedes what they produce in training. On the flip side, this is also why a golfer struggles to **'take their range game to the golf course.'**

6 – Golf Practice
Motivation Trumps All, While Confidence Can Be A Killer

Which of these do you think is more important for a golfer to possess – confidence or motivation?

If we describe motivation as the direction and intensity of your effort, we can hypothesize that the absence of motivation (or the presence of the wrong type of motivation) makes pretty much everything you've read so far worthless.

Motivation allows you, the golfer, to take advantage of two remarkable gifts – the physical and mental adaptability that all humans possess.

Mental adaptations and physical change to your movements will synergize and result in you playing better golf – but only if you are motivated to engage in the tasks you have read in this book. In fact, we'd go so far as to say that this book will not make you a better golfer – the effective practice of the exercises we've shared with you is what will make you a better golfer.

To help you better understand motivation, and how vital it is to your improvement, let's look at the 3 forms of motivation: zero, extrinsic and intrinsic.

Zero motivation is a critical state, as without motivation you have nothing at all driving you. If you lack any level of motivation, then simply maintaining your performance is not possible. As time passes, you will slide off the treadmill to a place where going through the motions barely does justice to the sheer extraordinary mass of your apathy. You are, we're sorry to say, going nowhere – and we'd be surprised if you've even reached this part of the book.

Extrinsic motivation, on the other hand, does result in any kind of athlete directing their efforts towards achieving the results they desire. It is, by dint of actually existing, far better than zero motivation. However, research confirms that athletes that focus on results and external rewards often fail to develop the resilience and character of those that are intrinsically motivated.

Intrinsic motivation directs your efforts towards constant self-improvement, creating a deeper desire and purpose that, as the 'Sports Guys' say 'burns' within the athlete. More tellingly, research concludes that this form of motivation equips an athlete with character traits such as resilience and a growth mindset. And it is this character that acts as the ferocious V8 engine that drives an individual to succeed.

Basically, extrinsic forms of motivation can catalyze change but are finite. Sustainable motivation comes from an intrinsic source.

So, if you really want to get better at golf you must look deep inside and ask yourself why?

This intrinsic motivation should be more powerful than any trophy. Telling some golfers this is like convincing a buffalo he is crocodile-proof.

But if we look at the greatest athletes that have ever lived this appears to be true. The trophy is simply a reminder of all the effort that went into that achievement. The trophy is incidental, the actual effort of applying and sticking to a process is where true fulfillment lies.

Let's look at a man who's used to arriving first, Usain Bolt. Bolt, and many of his fellow sprinters are often regarded as 'genetic freaks' or 'naturals' rather than highly motivated human beings with the same broad genetic structure as those of us who could not run for a bus.

At the 2008 Olympic Games in Beijing, we all watched in awe as the comparatively tiny island of Jamaica captured six gold medals in track and field, and 11 overall. Usain Bolt won both the Men's 100 and 200 meter races, setting new world records in the process.

A relatively poor and undeveloped nation of just 2.8 million people – 1% the population of the United States – somehow managed to produce the fastest human alive.

One particularly unsatisfactory assessment seemed to find a substantial voice. Usain Bolt was a genetic freak. And this wasn't just a mantra for the ill-informed. Respected geneticists and science journalists have likened Bolt to a 'genetic secret weapon'.

Biologically, it turns out that almost all Jamaicans are flush with alpha actinin-3, a protein that drives forceful, rapid muscle contractions. This remarkably powerful protein is produced by a speed gene variant called ACTN3, at least one of which can be found in 98% of Jamaicans – far higher than in many other ethnic populations. Leading many to conclude that Bolt's gold medals were, in actual fact, a victory for his genetic make-up.

Not quite. As is often the way in the rush to marvel at extraordinary human achievement, no one actually stopped to do some fairly rudimentary math. 80% of Americans also have at least one copy of ACTN3 – adding up to a-none-too-shabby 240 million people. 82% of Europeans have it as well – landing us with another 597 million potentially extraordinary sprinters. At least 837 million people in the world that we know of had the same genetic capacity as Usain Bolt and yet he is the one with the medals. Why? To put it almost embarrassingly simply, because Jamaican's love to sprint and are intrinsically motivated to do so!

You may firmly believe that there must have been some other, more exclusive, genetic advantage that has not been discovered yet. You may well be right. You may well, like those sharp-minded fellows who thought the earth was flat or the sun was a malevolent fire god, be horribly wrong.

Genetics absolutely play some role in an athlete's journey to excellence. However, without motivation, genetic gifts can be compared to a Formula One car driven by your gran. Motivation is the driving force to elite performance and is ignited by the environments we are exposed too.

Much to the surprise of my high school math teacher, let me close this argument with a few equations. Imagine that athletic potential can be expressed through the following sums.

Athletic potential = genetics
This represents a fixed mindset and, if you want to improve (and this is your view of the world) it will be tough as you have already put a ceiling on your development.

Athletic potential = genetics + environment
This equation understands that environment plays a part in talent development but does not understand the extent of its influence. The environment plays a far more powerful role in evolving golfing performance.

Athletic potential = genetics x environment
Above is the view that not only is the environment playing a role, it is having a huge impact on athletic development. Represented by the impact of changing it from an additional factor to a multiplying one.

So, returning to our fundamental question, what exactly does an athlete need to be great? Motivation is a prerequisite if you are going to take the information in this book and turn it into golfing performance.

Be motivated to create a training environment that enables you to train to learn, train to perform but, most importantly, embraces failure as this will help you find future successes. Fuel this training environment with a deep connection to why you want to practice and why you desire to improve your golfing performance.

But, while we can't possibly say enough about the importance of motivation we are (brace yourselves sports fans, coaches, players, journalists and pundits all over the world) not all that bothered about confidence.

Our view is this. You don't actually have to go in search of confidence to be the best you can be at golf. There seems to be a societal norm and belief in the sports world that the super confident guy is the one that will prosper. This is simply not the case. Especially for the majority of golfers who are going to be reading this book.

The super confident golfer already knows what to do, they didn't read this book, why would they, they are, after all, super confident.

The super confident golfer doesn't need to practice, practicing is weak. Why practice when you can already win without even trying?

Ask them to smack a 250-yard 3-wood over water into the breeze and they'll throw back their super confident head and laugh in our doubtful little faces. After all, if they've managed to carry the same precise shot hundreds of times on the range, what is there to fear?

Ok, so that example is a little flippant, but the point is this – don't go looking for confidence. As humans we are designed to doubt, designed to think negatively, designed to pay attention to threatening stimuli. And this can be a good thing for performance – if we embrace it.

Understand the nerves that we feel on the golf course are a good thing, they can help us pay attention to the things that matter in our game, like not thinking we can hit our 3-wood 250-yards over water because we did it once in practice and selecting a more appropriate shot.

Rather than go in search for confidence, if you truly want to get better at golf look to improve **self-efficacy** or rather the belief you have in your own to ability to achieve goals. (The legendary psychologist Albert Bandura defines it as a personal judgement of *'how well one can execute courses of action required to deal with prospective situations'.*)

But how can you begin to grow your own capacity for self-efficacy? By setting process goals.

The power of a process goal
We live in a result obsessed world. Golfers are conditioned to think 'if I shoot this score I will win the tournament. If I win the tournament my ranking will increase. If I get a good ranking I will make it as a tour pro. If I am a tour pro I will be disgustingly rich' and so on. Here the outcome focus is winning, the ranking and becoming a tour pro. The external motivation is wealth.

This may be the dominant social and cultural thought that surrounds all aspects of our lives, yet we know at a fundamental level it is an illusion.

If you are a golfer that believes your next actions would determine the success or failure of your entire golf future how would you react? We're not ashamed to say we'd react with something approaching blind terror. Our heart rate would increase, our hands would tremble and, most unpleasantly for all of us, we'd be sweating like a bear, all resulting in low self-efficacy.

If you can move away from this kind of outcome focus or external focus and focus on the **process** of constant self-improvement, and the effective practice of the tasks in this book, your levels of self-efficacy will inevitably increase.

So, in other words, there's no value in becoming a confident golfer. The true value is in the quest to develop self-efficacy and intrinsic motivation through creating a Game Like Training environment for your practice.

7 – Golf Practice
Making PAR

We all know plenty of golfers who would swap a moderately well-loved nephew to shoot par during the monthly medal.

But there is a very different kind of par we should be aiming for while we practice – PLAN, ACT and REFLECT.

Plan

Plan the session, have a clear goal for what you want to achieve, the specific interleaved circuit, performance game or on-course challenge that will take you a step closer to this goal.

When training to learn, every ball we hit should have a clear, movement-oriented goal. When we action this goal, we must disassociate ourselves with the outcome of the shot and become focused solely on accessing the desired movement.

When training to perform we must recreate and simulate situations we will face on the golf course. Use Game Like Training and on-course challenges and work towards achieving your personal best score.

Most of all, write down your 'why'. Why do you want to practice today? What drives you? What is keeping you out here in the wind and the rain while your friends are off having fun? Understand your 'why' and you understand what gives you fulfillment (and that is a pretty huge thing to understand).

Act

Keep your scores, write down notes as you practice, embrace failure as the wonderful opportunity to learn it really is.

Re-live the positives, remember what it feels like, sounds like, looks like when you get it right.

Reflect

Spend time reviewing your plan and your practice actions.

Make a realistic performance review and use this to plan your next session – create a self-regulation cycle that will help you decide *what* your next practice session will be and *how* you will achieve this.

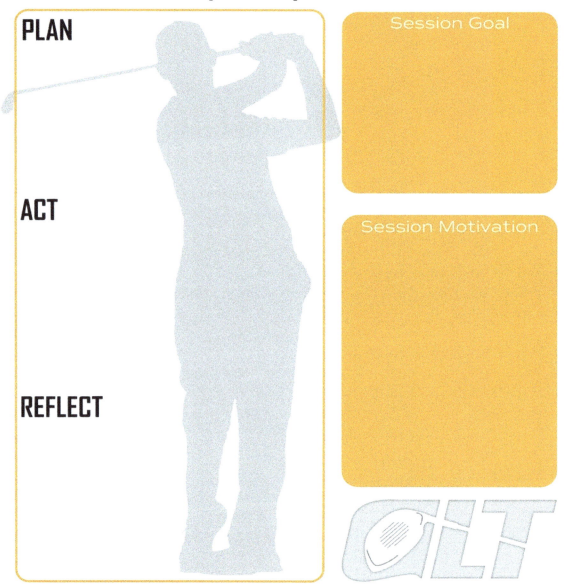

Download the above template at https://www.gltgolf.com/golf-coach-instructor-resource.html

88 | Game Like Training

Characteristics Of Psychological Excellence

The best golfers in the world all display different golf swing characteristics – cupped wrists, bowed wrists, strong grips, weak grips, across the line or laid off. All of this can be seen on the PGA Tour and is talked about and analyzed to death. But what is rarely discussed by Faldo, Chamblee, Pugh and all the other TV pundits is this…

How did this elite athlete practice to learn and retain this swing?

What practice environments did this player become exposed to or create that enabled them to adapt to the environment and transfer their skills to the golf course?

What was present in this athlete's social background that motivated and inspired them to stick to the process of constant self-improvement and deal with adversity?

One simple reason that discussions on *what* the club is doing as it travels around the body happen more often than *how* this is achieved is we can easily see and measure the golf swing. The psychological habits of excellence that drive retention and transfer of these skills are immeasurable.

Let's check out Ricky Fowler, a gentleman of the game who has managed to retain swing changes and transfer them into some of the most stressful environments in professional golf.

Disclaimer – none of us at GLT have ever worked with Ricky Fowler, nor do we know him personally. We wish we did because he's awesome and we would love to chill out in Jupiter eating oysters and drinking Red Bull with this magnificent orange man. Not that we're needy or anything.

What we do know is this – as a child Ricky was a motocross rider. Motocross is a sport where if you make a mistake, there are often very painful consequences.

If you don't develop the psychological habits of excellence that keep you calm during contextual and stressful practice as you fling your bike around turns that resemble the hazards of a competitive track, then you better have good health insurance.

Or, of course, you could just take up a golf, a sport with a very different kind of practice environment – one where consequence and physical risk are virtually absent, and where the psychological urgency so vital to elite performance is bored into non-existence by the relentless ping, ping, ping, ping of the range.

How much of Ricky's motocross practice mindset transferred to his ability to **think differently** and **train differently** in his golf when compared to the thousands of mini tour players that can't quite do what he does on a regular basis – players, you could argue, have swings that show up on camera every bit as impressively as Rickie's.

At GLT we believe Fowler developed psychological habits of excellence from his exposure to this extreme sport. It's this psychological excellence that is the differentiating factor.

But don't panic, we're not suggesting you need to take up a dangerous sport or shatter a few bones in the pursuit of a better golf game.

What we are suggesting is that golfers across the globe could take a step closer to mastering this sport if they paid more attention to *how* the best in the world build their golf swings.

Unfortunately, environments that implicitly drive golfers to think differently and train differently are not measurable. There is no exact science to this. But we do hope that, as you finish this book, you can take some of our ideas into your golf practice that will create a new type of practice environment – one that helps you focus on *how* you will evolve your skills through the introduction of spacing, variability and challenge so you can make those swing changes stick.

Of course, we hope you're inspired to engage in the contextual performance games and on course challenges we've shared. But most of all we hope that this book can help **you** use golf practice as a vehicle to build psychological habits of excellence, such as a process focus and intrinsic motivation, you can use in other areas of your life.

We hope we've contributed something positive to your game. But we'd love to think we've contributed something positive to your life too.
See you out there.

GLT x

ABOUT THE AUTHORS

As a team of authors, it is not our goal not to be right, it's our goal to make people think and influence behaviors.

We wrote this book wanting to help golfers across the globe make more informed choices about how they spend their practice time, increase the chance of them transferring their range game to the course and, by extension, gain so much more pleasure out of this amazing sport.

Our aim has only ever been to make a positive contribution to the world of golf in an area we are extremely passionate about.

So please feel free to contact us with any questions you may have, and we will be happy to talk to you about what we're trying to do.

Many thanks,
Team GLT x

GLT Co-Founder – Iain Highfield ihighfield@gltgolf.com

Favorite quote: *'Tell me and I forget, teach me I may remember, involve me and I will learn'.*

Created a golf psychological conditioning program that was implemented at the Nike Golf Academy (UK) Bishops Gate Academy (FL) International Junior Golf Academy (SC).
Iain's golf psychology program is currently being delivered to Penn State University Students, European Tour Golfers and D1 College Golfers
Published author, 'OSVEA, Practical Ways to Learn Golf's Mental Game'
Key note speaker at the South African PGA show 2018 & U.S PGA show 2017 & 2016
Golf Digest online coach 2017, 2018, 2019
Named Golf Digest Top Young Coach 2017, 2018, 2019.
Consulted with companies such as Ping, K-Motion and other industry leaders on effective practice for golf

GLT Co-Founder – Matthew Cooke info@gltgolf.com

Favorite quote: *'You get out what you put in and sometimes not even that'.*

GB&I PGA Certified Golf Coach
Published author, *'Expert Golfer, the truths on how to become one.'*
Key note speaker at the South African PGA show 2018 & U.S PGA show 2016
Coached Professional Golfers on the Ladies European Tour
Consulted with European Tour coaches and players on effective practice for golf
Consulted with companies such as Ping, K-Motion and other industry leaders on effective practice for golf

Glt Advisor – Zach Parker zachparkergolf@gmail.com

Favorite quote: *'The key is not the will to win, everybody has that. It's the will to prepare to win that is important.'*

Gary Gilchrist Golf Academy - Director of Golf
Bishops Gate Golf Academy - Founder and Director of Performance
Coached members of the following international teams - Mexico, Peru, Columbia, Venezuela, Switzerland, France, Philippines, Hong Kong, Japan, England, Slovakia, Trinidad & Tobago Germany
GravityFit Consultant to PGA Tour Players and College Golf Teams
Coached players on the European Tour
Named Golf Digest Top Young Coach 2019

Glt Director – Arick Zeigel azeigel@gltgolf.com

Favorite quote: *'You do not rise to the occasion, you sink to the level of your training'*

Coached students who have received scholarships to the following colleges: Indiana University, University of Kansas, Western Michigan, University of New Mexico, University of Utah, Columbia University, Saint Leo University, Eastern Tennessee State, Kennesaw State, Samford University.

Guest Speaker at the U.S PGA Show 2018

PGA Class A Member

Penn State University - Biomechanics of Golf

K-Motion Level 2 Certified

SAM PuttLab Level 2 Certified

Assisted PGA Tour coaches Hank Haney, Kevin Smeltz & Dr. Robert Neal

BodiTrak Certified Ground Mechanics Specialist

Capto Level 2 Certified

UCCS PGA Golf Management Degree

UCCS Business Degree with an emphasis in Service Management

More GLT resources that can help you think differently, train differently and help you take your range game to the course:

Other Publications
Expert Golfer by Matthew Cooke
https://www.gltgolfstore.com/p/golf-books/glt-53399.html
OSVEA – Practical Ways To Learn Golf's Mental Game by Iain Highfield
https://www.gltgolfstore.com/p/golf-books/glt-osvea.html

Free Downloads
Swing Tips That Work by Zach Parker
https://www.gltgolf.com/golf-coach-instructor-resource.html
Golf Pre Shot Routine Guide by Iain Highfield
https://www.gltgolf.com/golf-coach-instructor-resource.html
A parent's role in organized sports by Iain Highfield
https://www.gltgolf.com/golf-coach-instructor-resource.html

GLT online certification Level 1
Become a level 1 certified GLT coach
https://www.gltgolf.com/golf-teacher-training/glt-golf-coach-training-schedule.html

Free Online Courses
Mental Game of Golf by Iain Highfield
https://www.gltgolf.com/golf-coach-certification/osvea-golf-mental-performance-online-course.html
Golf Motor Learning by Matthew Cooke
https://www.gltgolf.com/golf-teaching-certification-certification-programs/golf-motor-learning-teaching-certification.html

Golf Online Store
Golf store to purchase the training aids featured in this book such as GravityFit
https://www.gltgolfstore.com/c/golf-training-aids.html

CPSIA information can be obtained
at www.ICGtesting.com
Printed in the USA
BVHW020934231219
567575BV00026B/1245/P